The Civil War: The North

Thomas Streissguth, *Book Editor*

David L. Bender, *Publisher*
Bruno Leone, *Executive Editor*
Bonnie Szumski, *Editorial Director*
Stuart B. Miller, *Managing Editor*
David M. Haugen, *Series Editor*

Greenhaven Press, Inc., San Diego, California

Other Books in the History Firsthand Series:

The Civil War: The South
The Great Depression
Japanese American Internment Camps
Sixties Counterculture

Every effort has been made to trace the owners of copyrighted material. The articles in this volume may have been edited for content, length, and/or reading level. The titles have been changed to enhance the editorial purpose.

Library of Congress Cataloging-in-Publication Data

The Civil War: The North / Thomas Streissguth, book editor.
     p. cm. — (History firsthand)
    Includes bibliographical references (p.) and index.
    ISBN 0-7377-0363-6 (pbk. : alk. paper) —
    ISBN 0-7377-0364-4 (lib. bdg. : alk. paper)
    1. United States—History—Civil War, 1861–1865.
  2. Northeastern States—History—19th century. 3. United States—History—Civil War, 1861–1865—Social aspects. I. Streissguth, Thomas, 1958– . II. Series.

E468 .C62   2001
973.7—dc21   00-039401
                                                CIP

Cover photo: Digital Stock

Printed in the USA

Contents

Chapter 2: Fighting for the Union Cause

Chapter 3: In the Officer's Tent

Mexican War—skillfully maneuvers around Confederate units in southern Missouri.

Chapter 6: Doctoring for the North

Chapter 7: Appomattox and Victory

devotion to the Union cause and his desire to see the supporters of the Confederate cause punished.

3. Captain Adams Musters Out
Many soldiers looked forward to peacetime with hopefulness as well as anxiety. An officer bids farewell to army service and eagerly anticipates the return to a civilian's peaceful life.

4. Advice from an Old Friend
Violently reunited, the people of the United States, and liberated African Americans, now had to adjust to a new society. A Northern abolitionist offers guidance to the newly freed slaves of the South.

Foreword

In his preface to a book on the events leading to the Civil War, Stephen B. Oates, the historian and biographer of Abraham Lincoln, John Brown, and other noteworthy American historical figures, explained the difficulty of writing history in the traditional third-person voice of the biographer and historian. "The trouble, I realized, was the detached third-person voice," wrote Oates. "It seemed to wring all the life out of my characters and the antebellum era." Indeed, how can a historian, even one as prominent as Oates, compete with the eloquent voices of Daniel Webster, Abraham Lincoln, Harriet Beecher Stowe, Frederick Douglass, and Robert E. Lee?

Oates's comment notwithstanding, every student of history, professional and amateur alike, can name a score of excellent accounts written in the traditional third-person voice of the historian that bring to life an event or an era and the people who lived through it. In *Battle Cry of Freedom*, James M. McPherson vividly re-creates the American Civil War. Barbara Tuchman's *The Guns of August* captures in sharp detail the tensions in Europe that led to the outbreak of World War I. Taylor Branch's *Parting the Waters* provides a detailed and dramatic account of the American Civil Rights Movement. The study of history would be impossible without such guiding texts.

Nonetheless, Oates's comment makes a compelling point. Often the most convincing tellers of history are those who lived through the event, the eyewitnesses who recorded their firsthand experiences in autobiographies, speeches, memoirs, journals, and letters. The Greenhaven Press History Firsthand series presents history through the words of first-person narrators. Each text in this series captures a significant historical era or event—the American Civil War, the

Great Depression, the Holocaust, the Roaring Twenties, the 1960s, the Vietnam War. Readers will investigate these historical eras and events by examining primary-source documents, authored by chroniclers both famous and little known. The texts in the History Firsthand series comprise the celebrated and familiar words of the presidents, generals, and famous men and women of letters who recorded their impressions for posterity, as well as the statements of the ordinary people who struggled to understand the storm of events around them—the foot soldiers who fought the great battles and their loved ones back home, the men and women who waited on the breadlines, the college students who marched in protest.

The texts in this series are particularly suited to students beginning serious historical study. By examining these firsthand documents, novice historians can begin to form their own insights and conclusions about the historical era or event under investigation. To aid the student in that process, the texts in the History Firsthand series include introductions that provide an overview of the era or event, timelines, and bibliographies that point the serious student toward key historical works for further study.

The study of history commences with an examination of words—the testimony of witnesses who lived through an era or event and left for future generations the task of making sense of their accounts. The Greenhaven Press History Firsthand series invites the beginner historian to commence the process of historical investigation by focusing on the words of those individuals who made history by living through it and recording their experiences firsthand.

Introduction

In the early morning hours of April 13, 1861, after withstanding an artillery bombardment lasting more than twenty-four hours, a small garrison of U.S. troops under the command of Major Robert Anderson raised a white flag of surrender over Fort Sumter, an island fortress lying in the harbor of Charleston, South Carolina. Anderson's troops marched out of the fortress and into captivity, having just survived the first engagement of the four-year conflict known as the Civil War.

The firing on Fort Sumter sparked feelings of anger and patriotism among the people of the northern United States. Yet many Northerners had expected this bombardment, or something like it, for several months. The country was splitting into two separate nations, Union and Confederacy, North and South, over the issues of states' rights and slavery. Even as the Southern states left the Union after the election of President Abraham Lincoln in November 1860, Northern opinion remained divided over the issue of secession. But the attack on Fort Sumter united most of the North behind the goal of returning the South to the Union at the cost of war.

Many historians consider the Civil War the most important event in the history of the United States. It was responsible for the worst death and destruction in the country's history. The war temporarily resolved a long and bitter debate over the balance of power between state and federal governments, ended more than two hundred years of slavery, destroyed the Confederacy, and fostered lasting suspicion and misunderstanding between the North and the South.

There was no single, simple cause of the war. It was fought after many years of bitter argument between the North and the South over the issue of states' rights, of which

slavery was the most visible aspect. Together, the partici-
pants were struggling to resolve a problem no less important than the final form of the republic and the true meaning
of its Constitution.

The Distant Roots of War

The Civil War had many of its roots in the rapid growth and
industrialization of the United States in the early nineteenth
century. The dramatic changes taking place caused strains
within an increasingly diverse population—strains that had
their full expression in the U.S. Congress. Elected representatives of the eastern states viewed the increasing power
of western territories with alarm, where the people resisted
the idea of a strong, centralized federal government. Legislators from the South, a largely agricultural region, came to
distrust their colleagues from the urban, manufacturing-
based society of the North and grew increasingly sensitive
and hostile over the opposition of many Northerners to the
South's "peculiar institution" of slavery.

Southerners had good cause to worry. In the Northern
states, a growing abolitionist movement was arguing for outright emancipation of the slaves throughout the country—
an action that would deal a devastating blow to Southern
planters who depended on slave labor. The issue moved
westward with settlement, while both the North and the
South, slave owners and abolitionists, sought allies in the
western territories.

The slavery controversy worsened in 1819, when the Missouri Territory applied for statehood. Missouri's state constitution allowed slavery, but Northern congressmen opposed admission on other grounds: They believed it would
strengthen the Southern faction of Congress. The Missouri
Compromise of 1820 allowed Missouri into the Union as a
slave state but prohibited slavery in all new territories lying
north of 36' 30" latitude—the new state's southern bound-
ary. To provide balance among slave-state and free-state representatives in Congress, Maine was admitted to the Union
as a free state.

The issue of slavery gradually became the focus of the increasingly bitter dispute between the North and the South over states' rights. Northern abolitionists published strident antislavery tracts and magazines; William Lloyd Garrison's newspaper the *Liberator* called for direct action by Northerners to free the slaves. Northerners helped slaves escape along the Underground Railroad, a string of safe houses that sheltered fugitives during their flight to Canada and out of the reach of bounty hunters bent on capturing and returning them to the South. To fight the Underground Railroad, Southern congressmen helped write and pass the Fugitive Slave Act in 1850. Under this law, anyone helping a slave escape was subject to a fine and a jail sentence. The Fugitive Slave Act sparked a great outcry among abolitionists in the North. Soon after it was passed, Northern state legislators retaliated with Personal Liberty Laws, which banned state officials from arresting or helping to arrest any fugitive slaves.

The Fugitive Slave Act and the Personal Liberty Laws sharpened the antagonism between the North and the South. Southerners held that the states had rights over and above the powers of the federal government in Washington. Northerners favored a strong and centralized government in which federal law was supreme. Such a government would prevent the chaos that would result from the states passing conflicting laws on the whim of their own legislatures. Northerners also expressed disdain at the plantation system of the South and dismay over the institution of slavery, which belied the promises of individual rights and liberty embodied in the Constitution; meanwhile, Southerners saw their economy and way of life threatened by interfering abolitionists.

When California applied for statehood in 1850, another compromise was reached: The inhabitants of each territory would decide for themselves whether to permit slavery. The Kansas-Nebraska Act of 1854 followed this doctrine in two new western territories. Nebraska, settled by a majority of "free-soilers," was admitted as a free state and remained peaceful. Kansas, however, became a violent battleground between slave owners and abolitionists, both of whom settled in the state in order to claim it for their respective sides.

In reaction to the Kansas-Nebraska Act, a new political party appeared in the North. The Republican party, founded in Ripon, Wisconsin, in 1854, stood for a strong federal government and the prohibition of slavery in new territories and states. The party steadily gained strength among Northern voters, who saw the Democratic party as the party of Southern and proslavery interests.

Soon after the presidential inauguration of a Northern Democrat, James Buchanan, the Supreme Court also weighed in on the slavery issue. In the case of *Dred Scott v. Sandford*, the Court had to decide whether a slave who entered a free state could sue for his release. The court decided against Dred Scott on the basis that slaves could not be citizens with the same rights as free persons. With this decision, the Supreme Court ruled that the U.S. Congress did not have the authority to prohibit slavery in new territories. Therefore, the Missouri Compromise was unconstitutional because it prevented slave-owning citizens the full use of their property—slaves—in free territory.

The First Shots of the War

The *Dred Scott* decision was the harbinger of the final irrevocable split between the North and the South. According to many historians, the first shots of the Civil War were fired on October 16, 1859, when the abolitionist John Brown led a raid on the federal arsenal at Harpers Ferry, Virginia (now West Virginia). Intending to spark an uprising against Southern slave owners that would bring down slavery once and for all, Brown fought off armed and determined townspeople as well as a company of federal troops under the command of Robert E. Lee. After his capture, Brown was tried in a Virginia court and was swiftly executed. While Southerners saw Brown as a fanatic and a murderer, many Northerners praised him as a hero and martyr for fighting for his beliefs in deeds, not words, against the institution of slavery.

The future battle lines dividing the North and the South rapidly took shape after Abraham Lincoln, candidate of the Republican party, won the presidential election of November 1860. After his victory, Lincoln clearly restated the platform adopted by the Republican party before the election: He favored a reversal of the *Dred Scott* decision and a ban on slavery in new territories. But he also pledged not to interfere with slavery in states that permitted it.

Lincoln's strategy was to limit the spread of slavery and see it gradually die out in the states where it remained legal. Among the people of the South, however, this policy represented an outright attack on their economy and their way of life. Fearing that new federal laws and Supreme Court decisions would turn against them under a Lincoln administration, Southern legislatures began seceding from the Union. On December 20, 1860, South Carolina passed the Ordinance of Secession, declaring itself free and independent of the United States. South Carolina was followed by Mississippi, Florida, Alabama, Georgia, Louisiana, and Texas. In February 1861 Southern leaders met in Montgomery, Alabama, to establish the Confederate States of America and to elect Jefferson Davis as their president.

The North could not permit the South to secede. Northerners saw the act of secession as a rebellion that, if allowed to succeed, would break the United States into two hostile nations doomed to fight endless conflicts over territory, trade, and ideology. If the Southern states had the right to secede, Northerners argued, then so did any state or region of the country. Eventually, the United States would simply disintegrate as individual states went their own way to pursue their own interests. Northern politicians, editorialists, and business leaders warned of future conflicts over the slave trade with Africa, over the ownership of new territories in the west, over foreign trade with Canada, Mexico, and Europe, and over fugitive slaves.

Most Northerners felt confident that their greater population (about 19 million, compared to the South's free population of 5.5 million), more advanced industry, and modernized transportation network would allow them to prevail in a war against the South. Some Northerners, however, warned that a fight to bring the South back into the Union would be difficult. The South had only to defend its territory while the North would have to attack and defeat the South and force an unconditional surrender. If that were accomplished, federal armies would then have to occupy the South, perhaps for decades, to support loyal state governments and to restore the Union.

After the secession of the Confederate states, federal fortifications, arsenals, and navy yards throughout the South were seized by Confederate units. One of the last holdouts was Fort Sumter, lying on an island within the busy harbor of Charleston, South Carolina. It was to Fort Sumter that several batteries of artillery, under the command of officers now loyal to the Confederacy, turned their attention in the early spring of 1861.

The interior of Fort Sumter is shown after its bombardment by Confederate troops. Fort Sumter was the last arsenal in the South to fall to the Confederacy.

The Call to Arms

The bombardment of Fort Sumter helped unite Northerners in the Unionist cause. But the overconfidence of the people could be seen in the federal government's lack of preparation for the upcoming war. The regular U.S. Army, with less than twenty thousand troops, was unprepared to fight a long war, and it was facing a Confederate force that had already been recruiting volunteers for a month.

To raise new troops, Lincoln issued a proclamation on April 15, 1861, calling on the states to provide a total of seventy-five thousand volunteers, who would serve a term of three months. On May 3, Lincoln called for forty more volunteer regiments and asked that forty thousand soldiers and sailors enlist for three-year terms in the regular army and navy. In a special session of Congress, convened on July 4, the president was authorized to recruit five hundred thousand men, who would serve for the duration of the war in the U.S. Army.

The enlistment drive was carried out in cities and towns throughout the North and was answered by young men expecting an easy three-month adventure of marching, camping, and occasional spirited fighting. In small towns and large cities, groups of fifty or one hundred men formed up companies and elected lieutenants or captains to lead them. They were thrown together with ten other companies to form a regiment and were then placed on a train for Washington, D.C., where they settled into training camps and took their appointed places in the hastily formed Army of the Potomac. Although career officers of the U.S. Army led some of the regiments, many of the commissions were granted to inexperienced or incompetent men as favors by Lincoln or state governors. In some cases, the newcomers outranked regular army officers with years of experience in the field.

While the Army of the Potomac trained, a general plan of military action was devised by General Winfield Scott, commander of the U.S. Army, in cooperation with Lincoln. The navy would blockade Southern ports, thus cutting off the Confederacy's vital cotton trade as well as supplies of arms and ammunition from foreign nations. The Union army would then attempt to divide the Confederacy by seizing the Mississippi valley. Eventually, as the Confederate armies weakened from the attrition of battle and from lack of supplies, the Union would advance to the south, attack the Confederacy's major industrial and rail centers, and seize its capital of Richmond, Virginia. The plan required time and patience, but the Northern public, confident of a quick victory, was clamoring for action.

Although Northern volunteer regiments were still receiving their first training, Lincoln gave the public what it wanted. The Army of the Potomac was marched across the Potomac River and into Virginia, into Confederate territory, in July 1861, just three months after the firing on Fort Sumter. The Union and Confederate armies fought their first battle near the town of Manassas and a small river called Bull Run. Untrained soldiers and officers became dazed and disoriented as the smoke of artillery fire and the scattering of horses created a scene of mass confusion. Eventually, the superior battlefield maneuvering of the Confederate generals, and the heroic stand of Confederate general Thomas "Stonewall" Jackson, won the day. The Union armies withdrew in disorder, accompanied by hundreds of civilians from Washington who had come to watch the battle as if attending a Sunday picnic.

The Battle of Bull Run provided a wake-up call for the Northern public and for the Lincoln administration. It became evident that the war would not be won so easily after all, that more troops were needed, and that the industry, foreign trade, and agriculture of the North must be completely turned to support the war effort. For the South, however, the victory at Bull Run created a fatal overconfidence on the part of military leaders and President Jefferson Davis. Instead of pursuing the victory and attacking Washington, D.C., the Confederate army stood its ground in Virginia. The Confederate government kept an embargo on cotton exports to Europe, believing that this would eventually force the European nations to extend diplomatic recognition to the Confederacy. While the North continued to make its preparations for war, the South missed its best chance for victory by staying on the defensive for another year.

Transformation of Industry and Agriculture

The secession of the eleven Confederate states had an economic impact on the North as well. Northern businesses found their trade with the South suddenly cut off. Many Northern banks that had made loans to Southern businesses failed, and trading firms that dealt in Southern crops such as tobacco and cotton lost money or closed their doors for good. Having lost the South's tax revenue, the U.S. government found itself in debt, unable to pay the banks and private investors that had loaned it money. The banking and business crisis caused a panic among investors as well as rising inflation; unemployment worsened as businesses closed their factories, fired their workers, and refused to hire new ones.

To deal with the financial crisis, the government passed the Legal Tender Act early in 1862. This law allowed the federal government to print its own paper money (currency had previously been printed and issued by banks and by local governments). The act reduced inflation and restored confidence among investors and the public, as the government now required that the new money be honored wherever and whenever it was presented for payment.

Eventually, the war provided a strong economic stimulus to the North, which already produced and consumed far more than the largely agricultural and more sparsely populated South. Although some factories closed down, new ones were opened to meet the demands of the huge Union army (in Philadelphia alone, 180 new factories were built between 1862 and 1864). To meet the demands of the war, Northern shops turned out textiles and clothing, arms and ammunition, iron and steel, machinery, leather goods, locomotives, and ships. The government passed high tariffs (duties on imports from foreign nations) to protect Northern businesses from competition. Union ships protected Northern trading vessels from Confederate raiders who operated in the Atlantic Ocean.

The wartime boom also helped the development of new technologies, such as the sewing machine and the Gordon McKay machine, which automated the production of shoes. While laborers left their jobs to join the ranks of the Union army, nearly one million European immigrants arrived to take their places on factory floors. The production of coal, the basic source of energy and the most important heating fuel, rose steadily from 19 million tons in 1861 to 24 million tons in 1864. The war also proved a boon to oil drillers, who began refining kerosene for use as a lamp fuel and exporting crude oil by the millions of barrels. Lumber and mining companies benefited from generous government contracts. In the long run, the Civil War industrial boom played an important role in transforming the United States into an international economic power in the last decades of the nineteenth century.

Despite a shortage of labor, Northern farming also eventually benefited from wartime demands. Having long put off the purchase of new equipment such as mechanical reapers and mowers, Northern farmers now had good reason to invest: Their crops were bringing high prices at a time when the government had to supply the vast Union armies. In addition, a Union blockade of Southern ports prevented the Confederacy from exporting its crops, allowing Northern farms a much larger share of foreign markets than they had enjoyed before the war. New legislation also spurred the settlement of western territories sympathetic to the Union cause. The Homestead Act of 1862 granted farmers 160 acres of land to settle and cultivate in the new frontier states west of the Mississippi. By the end of the war, 25 million new acres of land were put into production, helping to bring in record harvests of wheat, wool, and corn.

An Early Stalemate

In the meantime, the Union and Confederate armies accomplished little on the battlefield. The South failed to follow up on its victory at Bull Run, and for a full year very little fighting was actually done. The Union commander, George B. McClellan, was content to fortify his positions near Washington and to endlessly drill the volunteer regiments, even as Northern newspapers demanded action. The first Union victories took place in the west, where in February 1862 the newly commissioned Ulysses S. Grant captured Fort Henry and Fort Donelson in Tennessee. Grant then won the costly Battle of Shiloh, which prevented a Confederate campaign against Missouri and secured most of the Mississippi River valley, as far south as the fortified town of Vicksburg, Mississippi, for the Union. In April 1862 a fleet of Union gunboats under Commodore David Farragut sailed up the Mississippi River from the Gulf of Mexico. The fleet anchored near New Orleans, which was abandoned by Confederate troops and quickly occupied by the Union. For the rest of the war, the port of New Orleans remained in Northern hands; after Farragut captured Baton Rouge and Natchez, the entire lower Mississippi valley, except for Vicksburg, was lost to the Confederacy.

In the early spring of 1862, McClellan was finally prompted to act by the impatience of Lincoln and by calls for action from Northern civilians. McClellan shipped the Army of the Potomac down to the peninsula lying east of the Confederate capital city, Richmond. After reaching the peninsula, however, McClellan moved slowly and cautiously, giving the Confederate army time to outmaneuver him and protect the capital. Several battles were fought in which neither Union nor Confederate generals achieved a decisive victory. Although McClellan, who was eventually forced to retreat, had lost twenty thousand troops during the Peninsula Campaign, the Confederate army also suffered heavy losses. But because the Union army already outnumbered the Confederates, it could sustain much higher casualties without losing its ability to fight and to undertake long campaigns.

Antietam and Gettysburg

During the Peninsula Campaign of 1862, Confederate president Jefferson Davis had appointed a new commanding officer, General Robert E. Lee. A brilliant and audacious tactician, Lee was a graduate of the U.S. Military Academy at West Point. He was also a native of Virginia, however, and although he was reluctant to fight against his government, he believed it was his duty to fight for the Confederacy. Upon his appointment by Davis, Lee was determined to pursue the Union army into the North, where he believed a successful campaign against Washington, D.C., would persuade the Union side to ask for peace terms. Lee crossed the Potomac into Maryland on September 7, 1862. Ten days later, he fought McClellan's army to a bloody stalemate at the Battle of Antietam. Having lost a quarter of his men, fearing a counterattack, and seeing his supply lines threatened by Union cavalry, Lee retreated to the South, and McClellan, as cautious as ever, refused to pursue the enemy. McClellan's failure prompted Lincoln to replace him with General Ambrose Burnside later that fall.

Seeing the standoff at Antietam as the opportune time to deliver an important blow to the Confederacy, Lincoln wrote and delivered the Emancipation Proclamation. The proclamation announced that, as of January 1, 1863, all slaves living within states in rebellion against the United States would be freed. (Slave states that remained loyal to the Union—Delaware, Kentucky, Maryland, Missouri, and West Virginia—were excepted.)

The Emancipation Proclamation further inspired the Northern war effort; it also sparked a wave of pro-Union sentiment in England and the rest of Europe. Combined with the Union victory at Antietam, this rising pro-Union sentiment persuaded the governments of France and England not to recognize the Confederacy. In addition, after the proclamation became official, thousands of slaves deserted the South to enlist in all-black Union regiments. While contending with the racism of officers and white troops, unequal pay, and a lack of arms, these black regiments proved their courage in several crucial battles.

The year 1863 was the turning point of the war. On May 2, 1863, General Grant began a siege of Vicksburg, which finally surrendered on July 4. The defeat of Vicksburg brought the entire Mississippi valley under Union control, splitting the Confederacy in half. Just the day before Vicksburg's fall, a seventy-five-thousand-strong Confederate army under Lee had been turned back after a three-day battle at Gettysburg, Pennsylvania, ending the Confederate threat to the North for good.

In the meantime, the Union blockade of Confederate ports was beginning to have its effect on the Confederate economy. A small force of tugboats, frigates, converted paddlewheelers, and gunboats patrolled more than three thousand miles of coastline, watching for blockade-running ships carrying cargoes of arms and ammunition. Small fleets of armed Union gunboats captured ports on the Gulf of Mexico and on the Atlantic Ocean, preventing the Confederacy from shipping its goods abroad. Although ineffective at certain points, the blockade and the capture of the Mississippi valley caused rising prices and a weakening Confederate economy, just as General Scott had planned in early 1861.

Life in the Field

Despite the war's gradual turn in favor of the Union, the enthusiasm and excitement felt by Union soldiers on their first enlistment was changing to weariness, fear, and cynicism as the war dragged on. The rush of volunteers eager for the adventure of war slowed to a reluctant trickle; to make up for the shortage of volunteers, the U.S. Congress passed the Military Conscription Act in 1863. This law required all men between the ages of twenty and forty-five to register for the draft. Each state was also given a quota of volunteer soldiers to fill. If a state did not meet its volunteer quota, draftees were called up for service. A draftee could have a substitute take his place or he could pay a three-hundred-dollar bounty. As a result of the bounty law, few members of the upper classes served in ordinary infantry regiments. (In addition, "bounty jumpers" in search of a good living could volunteer, collect an enlistment bonus, then desert, move to a new location under a different name, and collect another bounty.) The new draft laws created bitter opposition in places—usually eastern urban centers—where many people opposed the war or supported the Confederacy outright.

Most of the draftees and volunteers in the Union army were young men between eighteen and thirty years of age. Although eighteen was the minimum legal age to enlist, many younger boys arrived at the recruiter's desk claiming to be old enough to fight and were accepted with no further questions asked. Immigrants made up an important segment of the army, especially Germans, Irish, and Scandinavians; as the war continued, African American volunteers formed all-black regiments commanded by white officers. The pay for enlisted men was low—eleven dollars a month to start, later raised to sixteen dollars a month, plus a small clothing allowance. The army issued a single uniform suit, made of poor woolen material. The standard fighting weapon at the start of the war was the inefficient, muzzle-loading Springfield rifle, which had to be reloaded by hand with each shot.

The soldiers lived in encampments made up of hundreds of tents, each housing up to a dozen men, pitched closely together along temporary dirt streets. They drilled, marched, and fought on a meager diet of heavily salted meat, hardtack biscuits made from flour and water, beans, coffee, and sugar. When the weather was hot, the camps were infested with hordes of insects, and primitive latrines and heaps of garbage created unpleasant and unhealthy sights and smells. In winter, coats and blankets were issued and log huts were built to keep the soldiers warm, but life was still mostly lived outdoors, where there was little to protect them from the driving snow and freezing winds.

When he was not fighting, the Northern soldier was still suffering—from the intense boredom of drill and from the weariness of constant physical labor. Officers drilled their companies all day long to prepare them for action. The soldiers were instructed how to march in line, how to withstand a charge, how to fire in unison, and how to retreat in good order. They were also set to the tasks of digging trenches, raising officers' cabins, gathering and chopping wood, and clearing brush for encampments. On Sundays, they were given free time to do their laundry, read books or letters from home, attend religious services, or purchase goods from the sutler (dry-goods merchant), who offered tobacco, books, clothing, tools, and assorted knickknacks at high prices.

Sanitary conditions in military camps and hospitals were poor, and many soldiers feared nothing so much as lying in a hospital cot. Union doctors and nurses, often overwhelmed by the numbers of dying and wounded soldiers, had to work in hastily built field hospitals, which usually consisted of a few large tents. At first, only male volunteers were accepted as nurses at the front, but women also played a vital role in helping the sick and wounded. Clara Barton, a government clerk, was inspired by the suffering she saw at the Battle of Bull Run to volunteer as a nurse, going among the wounded and dying on the battlefields of Virginia to offer aid and comfort. After the war, Barton helped establish the American Red Cross.

The worst conditions of all were found in the prison camps, which grew larger and larger as the war continued. Union soldiers unlucky enough to be captured were herded into crowded and disease-ridden camps, where many had to suffer in the open with no shelter whatsoever. At the prison camp in Andersonville, Georgia, more than thirty thousand Union soldiers died, with survivors carrying on a life-or-death struggle among themselves over paltry food rations, tattered clothing and blankets, and a patch of muddy ground on which to rest.

The War Drags On

Despite Grant's victories and the success of the Union blockade, Northern enthusiasm waned in 1864 as the war dragged on, casualties mounted, and families lost loved ones to battle wounds and disease. Still exasperated and impatient with his commanding officers, Lincoln finally promoted Grant to commanding officer of the U.S. Army. Grant invaded Virginia in May and fought a series of bloody battles against Lee's Army of Northern Virginia. Slowly but steadily, Grant pushed Lee down to the vicinity of Richmond, but Union troops were thrown back after making a ferocious assault at the Battle of Cold Harbor. After this defeat, Grant ordered his army to dig in and reinforce its position. On June 20, his army laid siege to the city of Petersburg, a rail center just south of Richmond. Although Grant had lost more than fifty thousand troops in the summer of 1864, the Army of Northern Virginia was losing the war of attrition because it could not easily replace its casualties.

In the meantime, a Union force under the command of William T. Sherman was rampaging across northern Georgia, destroying homes, farms, and everything else in its path. Sherman finally captured Atlanta, a vital manufacturing center and railroad hub, on September 1, 1864. The South began to lose hope after suffering another setback in November: Lincoln was reelected president after promising to continue the war until the complete surrender of the Confederacy and the restoration of the Union.

Surrender and Victory

By early 1865, Sherman was fighting his way through South and North Carolina to link up with Grant in Virginia. On April 2 Grant captured Petersburg, and then the Army of the Potomac invaded and conquered Richmond. Caught between the armies of Grant and Sherman, Lee saw that his hungry and bedraggled army was trapped. On April 9, at Appomattox Courthouse, Virginia, Lee and Grant met to discuss and sign the terms of the Confederate surrender. Two weeks later another Confederate army surrendered at Raleigh, North Carolina. The war had ended, but not without one final tragedy: the assassination of Lincoln in Washington on April 14. John Wilkes Booth, an actor who sympathized with the South, saw the murder as a final act of vengeance against the tyranny of Lincoln and the North.

The cost of the war was high for both sides. The Union had lost 140,400 killed in action and 224,100 dead from accidents and disease. The Confederacy suffered about 165,000 dead, about 75,000 of them in battle. The war had cost the federal government about $3 billion for supplies, arms, and salaries; the debts taken on to pay for the war burdened the nation for many years to come. States that had seen fighting suffered heavy damage that took many years, sometimes decades, to repair. Millions of families had lost loved ones, and many others suffered the terrible uncertainty of not knowing the fate of a missing soldier.

The Results of the War

The vast Union army quickly disappeared in the months after the Confederate surrender. From one million men in the spring of 1865, the army shrunk to less than 200,000 by the end of the year. Nevertheless, the bitter divide between the North and the South continued for many years after the war, and many believe it continues to the present day. Northern armies occupied southern cities until new governments were installed that would abolish slavery and swear loyalty to the Union. These reconstruction governments were met with great hostility among Southerners, who resented the Northern "carpetbaggers" who had arrived to rule over them. The Emancipation Proclamation brought freedom, but not equality, for Southern blacks, who were still denied legal rights to landownership, voting, education, and occupation. It was not until 1877 that all of the former Confederate states had returned to the Union.

After the war, the North prospered thanks to a solid manufacturing base on which to build, but the South struggled. Northern cities continued to grow with the development of new industries. Transcontinental railroads linked the east and the west, allowing rapid western settlement and expanded trade for Northern businesses. The labor force was expanded by new immigrants, and the introduction of durable paper currency stimulated new investment. In the memory of Northerners, the pain and suffering of the war was lightened by the sentiment that the war had been fought and won for good and noble causes: the preservation of the Union and the end of slavery.

Chapter 1

Fort Sumter and the Outbreak of War

Chapter Preface

A fter the election of Abraham Lincoln as president in November, 1860, the Southern slaveholding states seceded from the Union one by one. The Confederate States of America (CSA) was established, with its capital in Montgomery, Alabama. It was questionable if the people of the North would support an all-out war to preserve the Union and destroy the Confederacy. Despite the South's defiant actions, a large faction of Northerners were against the abolition of slavery and thought the seceding states were within their rights. The test, President Lincoln and his military commanders believed, would come with the first attack on a Union installation by Confederate forces.

By March, 1861, all federal military outposts except Fort Pickens in Pensacola, Florida, and Fort Sumter in Charleston, South Carolina, had been seized without resistance by Confederate forces. Confederate leaders claimed that these forts, located in territory claimed by the CSA, should be under Confederate control. Lincoln decided to make a stand at Sumter, ordering a resupply of urgently needed provisions and telegraphing his intentions to the Confederate leaders at Montgomery. The final decision of whether or not to use force would be in their hands.

Events moved quickly in early April. Its supply lines cut, the garrison at Fort Sumter ran low on food. A group of Confederate officers arrived in Charleston to demand the surrender of the fort and its commander, Major Robert Anderson. Anderson replied that he would surrender in two days' time, when he expected his provisions to run out. Instead of waiting, the Confederate officers gave the order to open fire on Fort Sumter. The bombardment began in the early morning of April 12, 1861.

The firing on Fort Sumter had the effect on public opinion in the North that Lincoln hoped for and expected. The forced surrender of a garrison flying the Stars and Stripes prompted thousands of men to volunteer for military service. Northerners united behind the goal stated by Lincoln in his inaugural speech of March 4, 1861: "I hold that, in contemplation of the universal law and of the Constitution, the Union of these States is perpetual. . . ."

Preparing for War

Jacob D. Cox

The controversies surrounding the issues of slavery and states' rights led to the secession of several Southern states from the Union in the winter and spring of 1860–61. Southern legislators withdrew from the United States Congress, and a Confederate government began meeting in Montgomery, Alabama. The people of the Northern, nonslave states prepared themselves for open war with their former countrymen from the South. Although the crisis appeared serious, and fighting inevitable, many still hoped that some kind of compromise could be worked out.

Then, on April 12, several batteries of artillery under the control of Southern officers opened fire on Fort Sumter, a U.S. Army base in the harbor of Charleston, South Carolina. Major Robert Anderson, the commander of Fort Sumter surrendered the next day. The Civil War had begun. It was now up to the Northern states to muster volunteer regiments to shore up the small and neglected federal army. In his memoir, Jacob Cox of Ohio describes the role he played in the organization of Ohio troops in the turbulent days following Fort Sumter.

On Friday, the twelfth day of April, 1861, the Senate of Ohio was in session, trying to go on in the ordinary routine of business, but with a sense of anxiety and strain which was caused by the troubled condition of national affairs. The passage of "ordinances of secession" by one after another of the Southern States, and even the assembling of a provisional Confederate government at Montgomery, had

Excerpted from Jacob D. Cox, "War Preparations in the North," as reprinted in *Battles and Leaders of the Civil War*, vol. 1 (New York: Century, 1887–1888).

not wholly destroyed the hope that some peaceful way out of our troubles would be found; yet the gathering of an army on the sands opposite Fort Sumter was really war, and if a hostile gun were fired, we knew it would mean the end of all effort at arrangement. Hoping almost against hope that blood would not be shed, and that the pageant of military array and of a secession government would pass by, we tried to give our thoughts to business; but there was no heart in it, and the "morning hour" lagged, for we could not work in earnest, and we were unwilling to adjourn.

Suddenly a senator came in from the lobby in an excited way, and, catching the chairman's eye, exclaimed, "Mr. President, the telegraph announces that the secessionists are bombarding Fort Sumter!" There was a solemn and painful hush, but it was broken in a moment by a woman's shrill voice from the spectators' seat, crying, "Glory to God!" It startled every one, almost as if the enemy were in the midst. But it was the voice of a radical friend of the slave, Abby Kelly Foster, who, after a lifetime of public agitation, believed that only through blood could his freedom be won, and who had shouted the fierce cry of joy that the question had been submitted to the decision of the sword. . . .

The next day we learned that Major Anderson had surrendered, and the telegraphic news from all the Northern States showed plain evidence of a popular outburst of loyalty to the Union, following a brief moment of dismay. That was the period when the flag—*The Flag*—flew out to the wind from every housetop in our great cities, and when, in New York, wildly excited crowds marched the streets demanding that the suspected or the lukewarm should show the symbol of nationality as a committal to the country's cause. He that is not for us is against us, was the deep, instinctive feeling. . . .

First Drills and Uniforms

From the hour the call for troops was published, enlistments began, and recruits were parading the streets continually. At the capitol the restless impulse to be doing something military seized even upon the members of the Legislature, and a good many of them assembled every evening upon the east terrace of the State House to be drilled in marching and facing by one or two of their own number who had some knowledge of company tactics. Most of the uniformed independent companies in the cities of the State immediately tendered their services and began to recruit their numbers to the hundred men required for acceptance. There was no time to procure uniforms, nor was it desirable; for these companies had chosen their own, and would have to change it for that of the United States as soon as this could be furnished. For some days companies could be seen marching and drilling, of which part would be uniformed in some gaudy style such as is apt to prevail in holiday parades in time of peace, while another part would be dressed in the ordinary working garb of citizens of all degrees. The uniformed files would also be armed and accoutered, the others would be without arms or equipments, and as awkward a squad as could well be imagined. The material, however, was magnificent and soon began to take shape. The fancy uniforms were left at home, and some approximation to a simple and useful costume was made. The recent popular outburst in Italy furnished a useful idea, and the "Garibaldi uniform" of a red flannel shirt with broad falling collar, with blue trousers held by a leathern waist-belt, and a soft felt hat for the head, was extensively copied and served an excellent purpose. It could be made by the wives and sisters at home, and was all the more acceptable for that. The spring was opening and a heavy coat would not be much needed, so that with some sort of overcoat and a good blanket in an improvised knapsack, the new company was not badly provided. The warm scarlet color reflected from their enthusiastic faces as they stood in line made a picture that never failed to impress the mustering officers with the splendid character of the men. . . .

On the streets the excitement was of a rougher if not more intense character. A minority of unthinking partisans could not understand the strength and sweep of the great popular movement, and would sometimes venture to speak out their sympathy with the rebellion, or their sneers at some party friend who had enlisted. In the boiling temper of the time the quick answer was a blow; and it was one of the common incidents of the day for those who came into the State House to tell of a knock-down that had occurred here or there, when this popular punishment had been administered to some indiscreet "rebel-sympathizer.". . .

At Camp Dennison, Cincinnati

New battalions arrived from day to day, the cantonments were built by themselves, like the first, and the business of instruction and drill was systematized. The men were not yet armed, so there was no temptation to begin too soon with the manual of the musket, and they were kept industriously employed in marching in single line, by file, in changing direction, in forming column of fours from double line, etc., before their guns were put into their hands. Each regiment was treated as a separate camp with its own chain of sentinels, and the officers of the guard were constantly busy inspecting the sentinels on post and teaching guard and picket duty theoretically to the reliefs off duty. Schools were established in each regiment for field and staff as well as for company officers, and Hardee's "Tactics" was in the hands of everybody who could procure a copy. One of the proofs of the unprecedented scale of our war preparation is found in the fact that the supply of the authorized "Tactics" was soon exhausted, making it difficult to get the means of instruction in the company schools. The arriving regiments sometimes had their first taste of camp life under circumstances well calculated to dampen their ardor. The 4th Ohio, under Colonel Lorin Andrews, president of Kenyon College, came just before a thunderstorm one evening, and the bivouac that night was as rough a one as his men were likely to experience for many a day. They made shelter by placing boards from the fence-tops to the ground, but the fields were level and soon became a mire under the pouring rain, so that they were a queer-looking lot when they crawled out in the morning. The sun was then shining bright, however, and they had better cover for their heads by the next night. . . .

Camp Hardships

The first fortnight in camp was the hardest for the troops. The plowed fields became deep with mud which nothing could remove till steady good weather should allow them to be packed hard under the continued tramp of thousands of men. The organization of camp-kitchens had to be learned by the hardest experience also, and the men who had some aptitude for cooking had to be found by a slow process of natural selection, during which many an unpalatable meal had to be eaten. A disagreeable bit of information soon came to us in the proof that more than half the men had never had the contagious diseases of infancy. The measles broke out, and we had to organize a camp-hospital at once. A large barn near by was taken for this purpose, and the surgeons had their hands full of cases, which, however trivial they might seem at home, were here aggravated into dangerous illness by the unwonted surroundings, and the impossibility of securing the needed protection from exposure. The good women of Cincinnati took promptly in hand the task of providing nurses for the sick and proper diet and delicacies for hospital use. The Sisters of Charity, under the lead of Sister Anthony, a noble woman, came out in force, and their black and white robes harmonized picturesquely with the military surroundings, as they flitted about under the rough timber framing of the old barn, carrying comfort and hope from one rude couch to another. . . .

Early Maneuvers

Though most of our men were native Ohioans, we had in camp two regiments made up of other material. The 9th Ohio was recruited from the Germans of Cincinnati, and was commanded by Colonel Robert McCook. In camp, the drilling of the regiment fell almost completely into the hands of the adjutant, Lieutenant August Willich (afterward a general of division), and McCook, who humorously exaggerated his own lack of military knowledge, used to say that he was only "clerk for a thousand Dutchmen," so completely did the care of equipping and providing for his regiment engross his time and labor. The 10th Ohio was an Irish regiment, also from Cincinnati, and its men were proud to call themselves the "Bloody Tenth." The brilliant Lytle was its commander, and his control over them, even in the beginning of their service and near the city of their home, showed that they had fallen into competent hands. It happened, of course, that the guard-house pretty frequently contained representatives of the 10th, who, on the short furloughs that were allowed them, took a parting glass too many with their friends in the city, and came to camp boisterously drunk. But the men of the regiment got it into their heads that the 13th, which lay just opposite them across the railroad, took a malicious pleasure in filling the guard-house with the Irishmen. Some threats had been made that they would go over and "clean out" the 13th, and one fine evening these came to a head. I suddenly got orders from General Bates to form my brigade and march them at once between the 10th and 13th to prevent a collision that seemed imminent. The long-roll was beaten as if the drummers realized the full importance of the first opportunity to sound that warlike signal. We marched by the moonlight into the space between the belligerent regiments; but Lytle already had got his own men under control, and the less mercurial 13th were not disposed to be aggressive, so that we were soon dismissed, with a compliment for our promptness.

Lincoln's Message to Congress

Abraham Lincoln

In the early summer of 1861, the federal armies were mustering in the state capitols and around Washington. Northern industries were turning out ammunition, weapons, and uniforms, and the federal government was preparing a naval blockade of Southern ports. Confident and hopeful, the people of the North were waiting for the quick and decisive battle that would settle the Southern rebellion.

President Lincoln still saw a need and a duty to rally the citizens to the war effort. On July 4, 1861, he gave an eloquent speech to a joint session of the United States Congress. In the speech, Lincoln recalled the events of the four months since his inauguration. He also gave his reasons—historical, legal, and moral—for opposing the secession of the Southern states by force.

Fellow-citizens of the Senate and House of Representatives: Having been convened on an extraordinary occasion, as authorized by the Constitution, your attention is not called to any ordinary subject of legislation.

At the beginning of the present Presidential term, four months ago, the functions of the Federal Government were found to be generally suspended within the several States of South Carolina, Georgia, Alabama, Mississippi, Louisiana, and Florida, excepting only those of the Post Office Department.

Within these States, all the Forts, Arsenals, Dock-yards, Custom-houses, and the like, including the movable and sta-

---

Excerpted from Abraham Lincoln's address to a special session of Congress, July 4, 1861.

tionary property in, and about them, had been seized, and were held in open hostility to this Government, excepting only Forts Pickens, Taylor, and Jefferson, on, and near the Florida coast, and Fort Sumter, in Charleston harbor, South Carolina. The Forts thus seized had been put in improved condition; new ones had been built; and armed forces had been organized, and were organizing, all avowedly with the same hostile purpose.

The Forts remaining in the possession of the Federal government, in, and near, these States, were either besieged or menaced by warlike preparations; and especially Fort Sumter was nearly surrounded by well-protected hostile batteries, with guns equal in quality to the best of its own, and out-numbering the latter as perhaps ten to one. A disproportionate share, of the Federal muskets and rifles, had somehow found their way into these States, and had been seized, to be used against the government. Accumulations of the public revenue, lying within them, had been seized for the same object. The Navy was scattered in distant seas; leaving but a very small part of it within the immediate reach of the government. Officers of the Federal Army and Navy, had resigned in great numbers; and, of those resigning, a large proportion had taken up arms against the government. Simultaneously, and in connection, with all this, the purpose to sever the Federal Union, was openly avowed. In accordance with this purpose, an ordinance had been adopted in each of these States, declaring the States, respectively, to be separated from the National Union. A formula for instituting a combined government of these states had been promulgated; and this illegal organization, in the character of confederate States was already invoking recognition, aid, and intervention, from Foreign Powers. . . .

Dissolution or Blood

The Governor of South Carolina [was notified] that he might expect an attempt would be made to provision the Fort; and that, if the attempt should not be resisted, there would be no effort to throw in men, arms, or ammunition, without further notice, or in case of an attack upon the Fort. This notice was accordingly given; whereupon the Fort was attacked, and bombarded to its fall, without even awaiting the arrival of the provisioning expedition.

It is thus seen that the assault upon, and reduction of, Fort Sumter, was, in no sense, a matter of self defence on the part of the assailants. They well knew that the garrison in the Fort could, by no possibility, commit aggression upon them. They knew—they were expressly notified—that the giving of bread to the few brave and hungry men of the garrison, was all which would on that occasion be attempted, unless themselves, by resisting so much, should provoke more. They knew that this Government desired to keep the garrison in the Fort, not to assail them, but merely to maintain visible possession, and thus to preserve the Union from actual, and immediate dissolution—trusting, as herein-before stated, to time, discussion, and the ballot-box, for final adjustment; and they assailed, and reduced the Fort, for precisely the reverse object—to drive out the visible authority of the Federal Union, and thus force it to immediate dissolution.

That this was their object, the Executive [President Lincoln] well understood; and having said to them in the inaugural address, "You can have no conflict without being yourselves the aggressors," he took pains, not only to keep this declaration good, but also to keep the case so free from the power of ingenious sophistry, as that the world should not be able to misunderstand it. By the affair at Fort Sumter, with its surrounding circumstances, that point was reached. Then, and thereby, the assailants of the Government, began the conflict of arms, without a gun in sight, or in expectancy, to return their fire, save only the few in the Fort, sent to that harbor, years before, for their own protection, and still ready to give that protection, in whatever was lawful. In this act, discarding all else, they have forced upon the country, the distinct issue: "Immediate dissolution, or blood."

And this issue embraces more than the fate of these United States. It presents to the whole family of man, the question, whether a constitutional republic, or a democracy—a government of the people, by the same people—can, or cannot, maintain its territorial integrity, against its own domestic foes. It presents the question, whether discontented individuals, too few in numbers to control administration, according to organic law, in any case, can always, upon the pretences made in this case, or on any other pretences, or arbitrarily, without any pretence, break up their Government, and thus practically put an end to free government upon the earth. It forces us to ask: "Is there, in all republics, this inherent, and fatal weakness?" "Must a government, of necessity, be too *strong* for the liberties of its own people, or too *weak* to maintain its own existence?". . .

It is now recommended that you give the legal means for making this contest a short, and a decisive one; that you place at the control of the government, for the work, at least four hundred thousand men, and four hundred millions of dollars. That number of men is about one tenth of those of proper ages within the regions where, apparently, *all* are willing to engage; and the sum is less than a twenty-third part of the money value owned by the men who seem ready to devote the whole. A debt of six hundred millions of dollars *now*, is a less sum per head, than was the debt of our revolution, when we came out of that struggle; and the money value in the country now, bears even a greater proportion to what it was *then*, than does the population. Surely each man has as strong a motive *now*, to *preserve* our liberties, as each had *then*, to *establish* them.

A right result, at this time, will be worth more to the world, than ten times the men, and ten times the money. . . .

It might seem, at first thought, to be of little difference whether the present movement at the South be called "secession" or "rebellion." The movers, however, well understand the difference. At the beginning, they knew they could never raise their treason to any respectable magnitude, by any name which implies *violation* of law. They knew their people possessed as much of moral sense, as much of devotion to law and order, and as much pride in, and reverence for, the history, and government, of their common country, as any other civilized, and patriotic people. They knew they could make no advancement directly in the teeth of these strong and noble sentiments. Accordingly they commenced by an insidious debauching of the public mind. They invented an ingenious sophism, which, if conceded, was followed by perfectly logical steps, through all the incidents, to the complete destruction of the Union. The sophism itself is, that any state of the Union may, *consistently* with the national Constitution, and therefore *lawfully,* and *peacefully,* withdraw from the Union, without the consent of the Union, or of any other state. The little disguise that the supposed right is to be exercised only for just cause, themselves to be the sole judge of its justice, is too thin to merit any notice.

With rebellion thus sugar-coated, they have been drugging the public mind of their section for more than thirty years; and, until at length, they have brought many good men to a willingness to take up arms against the government the day *after* some assemblage of men have enacted the farcical pretence of taking their State out of the Union, who could have been brought to no such thing the day *before*. . . .

The Constitution Challenged

What is now combatted, is the position that secession is *consistent* with the Constitution—is *lawful*, and *peaceful*. It is not contended that there is any express law for it; and nothing should ever be implied as law, which leads to unjust, or absurd consequences. The nation purchased, with money, the countries out of which several of these States were formed. Is it just that they shall go off without leave, and without refunding? The nation paid very large sums, (in aggregate, I believe, nearly a hundred millions) to relieve Florida of the aboriginal tribes. [After the Seminole War (1835–1842), in which four U.S. generals and 200,000 soldiers fought 3,000–5,000 Seminoles, nearly all of Florida's Indians were forcibly removed to the Indian Territory in the west.] Is it just that she shall now be off without consent, or without making any return? The nation is now in debt for money applied to the benefit of these so-called seceding

States, in common with the rest. Is it just, either that creditors shall go unpaid, or the remaining States pay the whole? A part of the present national debt was contracted to pay the old debts of Texas. Is it just that she shall leave, and pay no part of this herself?

Again, if one State may secede, so may another; and when all shall have seceded, none is left to pay the debts. Is this quite just to creditors? Did we notify them of this sage view of ours, when we borrowed their money? If we now recognize this doctrine, by allowing the seceders to go in peace, it is difficult to see what we can do, if others choose to go, or to extort terms upon which they will promise to remain.

The seceders insist that our Constitution admits of secession. They have assumed to make a National Constitution of their own, in which, of necessity, they have either *discarded,* or *retained,* the right of secession, as they insist, it exists in ours. If they have discarded it, they thereby admit that, on principle, it ought not to be in ours. If they retained it, by their own construction of ours they show that to be consistent they must secede from one another, whenever they shall find it the easiest way of settling their debts, or effecting any other selfish, or unjust object. The principle itself is one of disintegration, and upon which no government can possibly endure. . . .

This is essentially a People's contest. On the side of the Union, it is a struggle for maintaining in the world, that form, and substance of government, whose leading object is, to elevate the condition of men—to lift artificial weights from all shoulders—to clear the paths of laudable pursuit for all—to afford all, an unfettered start, and a fair chance, in the race of life. Yielding to partial, and temporary departures, from necessity, this is the leading object of the government for whose existence we contend.

I am most happy to believe that the plain people understand, and appreciate this. It is worthy of note, that while in this, the government's hour of trial, large numbers of those in the Army and Navy, who have been favored with the offices, have resigned, and proved false to the hand which had pampered them, not one common soldier, or common sailor is known to have deserted his flag.

Great honor is due to those officers who remain true, despite the example of their treacherous associates; but the greatest honor, and most important fact of all, is the unanimous firmness of the common soldiers, and common sailors. To the last man, so far as known, they have successfully resisted the traitorous efforts of those, whose commands, but an hour before, they obeyed as absolute law. This is the patriotic instinct of the plain people. They understand, without an argument, that destroying the government, which was made by Washington, means no good to them. . . .

It was with the deepest regret that the Executive found the duty of employing the war-power, in defence of the government, forced upon him. He could but perform this duty, or surrender the existence of the government. No compromise, by public servants, could, in this case, be a cure; not that compromises are not often proper, but that no popular government can long survive a marked precedent, that those who carry an election, can only save the government from immediate destruction, by giving up the main point, upon which the people gave the election. The people themselves, and not their servants, can safely reverse their own deliberate decisions. As a private citizen, the Executive could not have consented that these institutions shall perish; much less could he, in betrayal of so vast, and so sacred a trust, as these free people had confided to him. He felt that he had no moral right to shrink; nor even to count the chances of his own life, in what might follow. In full view of his great responsibility, he has, so far, done what he has deemed his duty. You will now, according to your own judgment, perform yours. He sincerely hopes that your views, and your action, may so accord with his, as to assure all faithful citizens, who have been disturbed in their rights, of a certain, and speedy restoration to them, under the Constitution, and the laws.

And having thus chosen our course, without guile, and with pure purpose, let us renew our trust in God, and go forward without fear, and with manly hearts.

On Opposite Sides

A. Nicholas and J.M. McCue

The sudden coming of war between North and South divided not only politicians and military leaders, but also communities, friends, and families. Soon after the firing on Fort Sumter, this exchange of letters took place between two acquaintances, Mr. A. Nicholas of New York City and Col. J.M. McCue, a civic leader and dedicated secessionist of Augusta County, Virginia.

McCue responds to Nicholas's anguished questions about secession and war by denouncing the hypocrisy and cowardly behavior of Northerners who did little to defend the country's honor against the British during the War of 1812. McCue taunts Nicholas further, writing that he would love to meet him in battle, but McCue knows that this is unlikely since Nicholas, like many other Northerners, would hire a mercenary to take his place.

B anking Office of A. Nicholas & Co.,
No. 76 Wall Street,
New York, 15th April, 1861.

Col. J. M. McCue,—Mt. Solon,—Dear Sir,

It is a long time since I had the pleasure of writing you of your health. I have been frequently informed by my friend Sibert who has been kind enough to advise me occasionally respecting Mt. Solon and yourself. We have in this city become highly excited by the news that Fort Sumter was fired into and taken by the troops of the Cotton [Southern] States.

Reprinted from letters between A. Nicholas and J.M. McCue reprinted in the *Staunton Spectator*, April 30, 1861.

The President's message, calling first for 75,000 troops and then increasing the demand to 175,000, has produced a profound and deep impression that we are about entering into an awful performance, the end of which no man can tell. The only hope now is, that Va. [Virginia] will stand firm by the Union and hold all the border States to the same line of policy—if she does, our misguided South Carolina friends can soon be brought to reason—if she does not, but goes to swell the triumphal car of secession, God knows the end. The universal sentiment here is, that if the Border States do go out, then the war must exterminate *the cause which has created* this contention. When I heard that South Carolina fired coolly and deliberately and wantonly upon our flag, I cried like a child, that our brothers should fire into us. If the men that did the deed would have seen the eyes that were dimmed, and the stout frames of strong men that shook when the news was received, they would have wished that the earth had swallowed them up. The newspapers and office seekers have done their best to set the sections against each other. May God forgive them I can't!—My Dear Sir, will Virginia secede? What is your opinion? Pray let me hear from you soon.

Yours,

A. Nicholas

Mt. Solon, 21st April, '61.

Mr. A. Nicholas—Dear Sir: Yours of the 15th inst. [this month], came to hand a few days ago. Circumstances that have occurred since, have *more* than answered one of the interrogatories you ask with so much apparent feeling, "Will Virginia secede?" She has not only seceded, but has on this morning, an army in the field, to defend our rights and institutions, that will carry terror to the hearts of those who vauntingly boast that they will "exterminate the cause," as you are pleased to term it, of all the difficulties between us. Could you, and the myrmidons [obedient warriors] of abolition, or agrarianism and all that is abominable in a free government, see, as I have had the opportunity within the past few days, the spirit of our people, your craven hearts would collapse within your cowardly carcasses. You who possess means to justify it, will send your *hired* mercenaries to overpower us, it may be. You may devastate our country, burn our towns, insult and abuse our women, but conquer us you can never do. When our brave and gallant sons are exterminated, if such could be, you will find our wives and daughters more than a match for all the Beechers, and Cheevers and Stowes [famous abolitionists] and that damnable set that you have so long paid Court to, and encouraged, until you have brought this affliction upon the country.

You speak of our "institutions" being the *cause* of this war, and you will exterminate it, forsooth. Let me tell you, sir, that it has been the misguided frenzy and folly and madness of your people, that has been the cause; and that people that has fattened and flourished upon the labor of this institution, and in your pharasaical [sanctimonious] and puritanical self-righteousness, after hoarding this wealth, would

The First Battle of Fort Sumter

According to tradition, the Civil War began with the bombardment of Fort Sumter in the early morning of April 12, 1861. However, the first shots of the war were heard three months earlier during a little-known incident in Charleston harbor, when a civilian merchant ship attempted to resupply the beleaguered garrison at Fort Sumter. In his book Best Little Stories from the Civil War, *C. Brian Kelly describes the action.*

The *Star of the West* arrived off the harbor entrance at 1:30 in the morning on January 9, then hove to in the main shipping channel to wait for daylight before proceeding further.

As daylight began to reveal her outlines, she was moving again. Artillery hidden in nearby sandhills opened fire. The first shot was traditional—across the bow. When the *Star of the West* kept moving, the cannon fire continued. Two rounds struck the merchant ship, which ran a flag up and down a forward mast as if a plea for Anderson to tell her what to do.

say to us, "stand aside, we are holier than thou," and cannot live under the same government with you. Let me say to you, sir, that the men of New York and New England who, in the war of 1812, could stand by with folded hands and see the flag of their country trailed and trampled in the dust, and convene themselves into a Hartford convention, and refuse to furnish men and means to defend their country and that flag from an insolent foreign foe, can with a very bad grace now shed tears, as you say you did, when you heard that flag was fired upon at Fort Sumter. Your damnable hypocrisy makes my blood boil, and in spite of myself, makes me pray that we may have the earnestly hoped for opportunity of meeting you in sight of the Potomac, and all those who, like you, have been shedding those crocodile tears, and there testing, in the sight of the ashes of the Father of his Country, your sincerity in defending that flag. But permit me to say, sir, that you will not be there. You, and those who think

---

Now Fort Moultrie lay in the ship's path, manned by hot-eyed Southern secessionists. And Moultrie's guns, while not yet in range, opened fire.

At Fort Sumter, all was confusion and disarray at the ship's unexpected appearance. Army surgeon Samuel Crawford, one of Major Anderson's seven officers at the island outpost, later wrote that Anderson didn't know what to do, since he had anticipated a warship rather than a merchant vessel. And further, snarled halyards prevented his men from replying quickly to the *Star*'s signals.

The *Star of the West* was not about to present her vulnerable broadside for a raking by the batteries at Fort Moultrie, and so the rescue ship turned and pointed toward the open sea. Major Anderson was about to order Fort Sumter's own guns into action—against Fort Moultrie. But he saw the ship turn away. "Hold on," he told his men. "Do not fire."

It was all over in just a few minutes.

C. Brian Kelly, *Best Little Stories from the Civil War.* Nashville, TN: Cumberland House, 1998.

like you, will send as your personal representatives, the miserable mercenary foreigners, that you can gather up in your cities at $10 per month to do your fighting. Would to God it were otherwise, and we could meet you all in person, and your boasted Seventh Regiment besides, who have warmed at our firesides, slept under our roofs, shared our hospitality, and when it was in your interest to do so, have preached up your conservatism. But enough, sir, I have not patience to say more. In the hope I may meet you at Washington, (what I do not expect,) I am, sir, yours.

J. Marshall McCue.

Panic at Bull Run

William H. Russell

In July, the long-awaited advance of the Union army into Virginia began. On July 21, a Union force under Major General Irvin McDowell attacked a Confederate army at Manassas Junction, Virginia, a short ride from Washington, D.C. Expecting excitement and a glorious victory for the Union, thousands of Washington residents turned out to witness the battle, many of them packing picnics for the occasion.

The cheering crowds would not have their victory, however. While skirmishing continued near a small river known as Bull Run, Confederate reinforcements arrived. McDowell's outmaneuvered army broke ranks and fled in a panicked retreat along the roads back to Washington.

Watching from a nearby hillside was English journalist William Russell. In the following excerpt, Russell describes the battle and the Union army's ignominious retreat.

The sounds which came upon the breeze, and the sights which met our eyes, were in terrible variance with the tranquil character of the landscape. The woods far and near echoed to the roar of cannon, and thin, frayed lines of blue smoke marked the spots whence came the muttering sound of rolling musketry; the white puffs of smoke burst high above the treetops, and the gunners' rings from shell and howitzer marked the fire of the artillery.

Clouds of dust shifted and moved through the forest; and, through the wavering mists of light blue smoke and the thicker masses which rose commingling from the feet of

Excerpted from William Russell's report of the Battle of Bull Run, July 1861.

men and the mouths of cannon, I could see the gleam of arms and the twinkling of bayonets.

On the hill beside me there was a crowd of civilians on horseback, and in all sorts of vehicles, with a few of the fairer, if not gentler, sex. A few officers and some soldiers, who had straggled from the regiments in reserve, moved about among the spectators, and pretended to explain the movements of the troops below, of which they were profoundly ignorant.

The cannonade and musketry had been exaggerated by the distance and by the rolling echoes of the hills; and sweeping the position narrowly with my glass from point to point, I failed to discover any traces of close encounter or very severe fighting. The spectators were all excited, and a lady with an opera glass who was near me was quite beside herself when an unusually heavy discharge roused the current of her blood—"That is splendid. Oh, my! Is not that first-rate? I guess we will be in Richmond this time tomorrow." These, mingled with coarser exclamations, burst from the politicians who had come out to see the triumph of the Union arms. I was particularly irritated by constant applications for the loan of my glass. One broken-down looking soldier, observing my flask, asked me for a drink, and took a startling pull, which left little between the bottom and utter vacuity.

"Stranger, that's good stuff and no mistake. I have not had such a drink since I come South. I feel now as if I'd like to whip ten Seceshers [secessionists]. . . ."

Notwithstanding all the exultation and boastings of the people at Centreville, I was well convinced no advance of any importance or any great success had been achieved, because the ammunition and baggage wagons had never moved, nor had the reserves received any orders to follow in the line of the army. . . .

Loud cheers suddenly burst from the spectators as a man dressed in the uniform of an officer, whom I had seen riding violently across the plain in an open space below, galloped along the front, waving his cap and shouting at the top of his voice. He was brought up by the press of people round his horse close to where I stood. "We've whipped them on all points," he cried. "We have taken all their batteries. They are retreating as fast as they can, and we are after them." Such cheers as rent the welkin! The Congressmen shook hands with each other and cried out, "Bully for us. Bravo, didn't I tell you so." The Germans uttered their martial cheers and the Irish hurrahed wildly. At this moment my horse was brought up the hill, and I mounted and turned towards the road to the front. . . .

A Surprising Retreat

I had ridden between three and a half and four miles, as well as I could judge, when I was obliged to turn for the third and fourth time into the road by a considerable stream, which was spanned by a bridge, towards which I was threading my way, when my attention was attracted by loud shouts in advance, and I perceived several wagons coming from the direction of the battlefield, the drivers of which were endeavoring to force their horses past the ammunition carts going in the contrary direction near the bridge; a thick cloud of dust rose behind them, and running by the side of the wagons were a number of men in uniform whom I supposed to be the guard. My first impression was that the wagons were returning for fresh supplies of ammunition. But, every moment the crowd increased, drivers and men cried out with the most vehement gestures, "Turn back! Turn back! We are whipped." They seized the heads of the horses and swore at the opposing drivers. Emerging from the crowd a breathless man in the uniform of an officer with an empty scabbard dangling by his side, was cut off by getting between my horse and a cart for a moment. "What is the matter, sir? What is all this about?" "Why it means we are pretty badly whipped, that's the truth," he gasped, and continued.

By this time the confusion had been communicating itself through the line of wagons toward the rear, and the drivers endeavored to turn round their vehicles in the narrow road, which caused the usual amount of imprecations from the men and plunging and kicking from the horses.

The crowd from the front continually increased; the heat, the uproar, and the dust were beyond description; and these were augmented when some cavalry soldiers, flourishing their sabers and preceded by an officer, who cried out, "Make way there—make way there for the General," attempted to force a covered wagon, in which was seated a man with a bloody handkerchief round his head, through the press.

I had succeeded in getting across the bridge with great difficulty before the wagon came up, and I saw the crowd on the road was still gathering thicker and thicker. Again I asked an officer, who was on foot, with his sword under his arm, "What is all this for?" "We are whipped, sir. We are all in retreat. You are all to go back." "Can you tell me where I can find General M'Dowell?" "No! nor can any one else."

A few shells could be heard bursting not very far off, but there was nothing to account for such an extraordinary scene. A third officer, however, confirmed the report that the whole Army was in retreat, and that the Federals were beaten on all points, but there was nothing in this disorder to indicate a general rout. All these things took place in a few seconds. I got up out of the road into a cornfield, through which men were hastily walking or running, their faces streaming with perspiration, and generally without arms, and worked my way for about half a mile or so, as well as I could judge, against an increasing stream of fugitives, the ground being strewed with coats, blankets, firelocks, cooking tins, caps, belts, bayonets, asking in vain where General McDowell was.

Cavalry Pursuit

Again I was compelled by the condition of the fields to come into the road; and having passed a piece of wood and a regiment which seemed to be moving back in column of march in tolerably good order, I turned once more into an opening close to a white house, not far from the lane, beyond which there was a belt of forest. Two fieldpieces, unlimbered near the house, with panting horses in the rear, were pointed towards the front, and along the road beside them there swept a tolerably steady column of men mingled with field ambulances and light baggage carts, back to Centreville. I had just stretched out my hand to get a cigar light from a German gunner, when the dropping shots which had been sounding through the woods in front of us suddenly swelled into an animated fire. In a few seconds a crowd of men rushed out of the wood down towards the guns, and the artillerymen near me seized the trail of a piece and were wheeling it round to fire when an officer or sergeant called out, "Stop! stop! They are our own men"; and in two or three minutes the whole battalion came sweeping past the guns at the double, and in the utmost disorder. Some of the artillerymen dragged the horses out of the tumbrils [cart harnesses]; and for a moment the confusion was so great I could not understand what had taken place; but a soldier whom I stopped, said, "We are pursued by their cavalry; they have cut us all to pieces. . . ."

There was nothing left for it but to go with the current one could not stem. . . . On arriving at the place where a small rivulet crossed the road, the throng increased still more. The ground over which I had passed going out was now covered with arms, clothing of all kinds, accoutrements thrown off and left to be trampled in the dust under the hoofs of men and horses. The runaways ran alongside the wagons, striving to force themselves in among the occupants, who resisted tooth and nail. The drivers spurred and whipped and urged the horses to the utmost of their bent. . . . As I rode in the crowd with men clinging to the stirrup leathers or holding on by anything they could lay hands on, so that I had some apprehension of being pulled off, I spoke to the men and asked them over and over again not to be in such a hurry. "There's no enemy to pursue you. All the cavalry in the world could not get at you." But I might as well have talked to the stones.

Chapter 2

Fighting for the Union Cause

Chapter Preface

The outbreak of the Civil War caught the U.S. Army unprepared. President Lincoln called up seventy-five thousand volunteers for military service, a call answered by boys and young men throughout the North. Many were farmers and small-town dwellers for whom military life represented an escape from a dull routine. The volunteers gathered in companies of one hundred, elected their leaders from among themselves, and drilled on courthouse lawns and open fields from Minnesota to Maine.

At first, army service meant no more than endless drilling and marching. As the Union generals dithered, bored volunteers sought what diversions they could in the huge encampments around Washington. Gambling, target shooting, carousing, and writing letters home held more interest for the volunteers than the movements of the Confederates. The war, they thought, would go quickly and easily, and might pass most men by completely.

Once led onto the battlefield, however, Union soldiers soon learned why they had been put through the weeks and months of close-order drill. Steeped in strategies of warfare designed for Napoleonic-era Europe, Union officers confronted the enemy by forming up units in neat double ranks, or lines. After claiming an open field or prominent hill, the unit offered battle with the front row kneeling, the back row standing, and officers in the rear to rally and regroup the men, if necessary. As the officers constantly reminded their soldiers, avoiding any gaps in the line was essential to success in battle and to the survival of the individual.

The southern United States was not Europe, however, and the terrain fought over was usually thickly forested and hilly—a terrain not always amenable to neat formations or to the coordination of military units in the field. As a result, battle for Union soldiers often meant confusion in the clouds of smoke and in the earsplitting noise of rifle and artillery fire. Thousands of soldiers might become separated from their units, and entire companies lost their way while maneuvering. In the shroud of smoke from battle the enemy might be confronted unexpectedly, resulting in hand-to-hand fighting of the grimmest sort.

The thrill of military life wore off quickly for many volunteers as the war dragged on. The boredom of life in camp and the dangers of battle discouraged many volunteers from re-enlisting, and eventually, to bring the Union army up to its needed strength, a draft was instituted in 1863. Although victorious, the Union army in the final months of the war was made up of hardy and weary conscripts and volunteers, all longing to return to a life of work, dull routine, and peace.

First Days in the Union Army

Rice C. Bull

Nineteen-year-old Rice Bull, along with a friend from Washington County, New York, answered President Lincoln's call for volunteers in June 1862, after a series of Union defeats. The volunteers were organized into the 123rd New York Infantry for a term of service to last three years. After mustering into the Union army at the town of Salem, they then shipped by train to Baltimore and Washington.

As Bull records in his memoirs, the recruits experienced boredom, exhaustion, discomfort, and sometimes hunger. They were drilled and marched repeatedly, and endlessly, in camp and in city streets. The wearying drills begin to exhaust his comrades, but, as Bull comes to realize, they also learn the discipline needed to carry them through the danger and confusion of future battles.

Before beginning the story of my experience as a Union Soldier during the Civil War, it might be well to tell of the conditions in our part of the country previous to my enlistment, as a boy of nineteen noted them in the spring of 1862. The war had started a year before and the period had been one of excitement and anxious waiting. We who lived on farms had no daily papers, only the weekly editions, so everyone who passed our house was questioned as to war news. At times we heard the distant sound of cannon at Whitehall or Glens Falls but the news, when details came,

Excerpted from the memoirs of Rice C. Bull, September–October 1862.

told either of a drawn battle or a defeat. Victories were few. We had met with so many military reverses that many feared that it would be impossible to reunite the country by force of arms. Thousands of boys like me felt a sense of duty to aid the Union cause for service in the Army. . . .

I had often thought of enlisting, believing it to be my duty, but until then no opportunity had come for me to do so. Before this time, most of the recruiting had been from the large towns far from the country districts. Now a regiment was to be raised in our own county, and it would consist mostly of farmers and farm boys.

A neighbor and school friend, Phineas Spencer, and I had agreed that we would go together and stand by one another. Spencer took action first by going to Fort Ann, where he enlisted; after that he came to me to go with him, as we had planned. My parents were at first loath to give their consent, but they realized that it was a call to duty that could not be disregarded. After grave and prayerful consideration, they tearfully consented to my going. I know now how hard it must have been for them to give their approval.

On August 13th, 1862 I worked with my father in the oat field until noon gathering the grain; that afternoon I went to Fort Ann and signed the papers that bound me to army service for three years, unless sooner discharged. I became a member of Company D, 123rd Regiment, New York Volunteer Infantry. That night I stopped at the Battle Hill Hotel in Fort Ann. The next morning, in company with several others who were to be my comrades, I took wagon for Salem where the Regiment was being organized and would camp until it was ordered to some place for preliminary training. . . .

I will not go into much detail of our stay in Salem. There were some attempts made at drilling but there was no parade ground as the field on which we were camped was small and nearly covered with tents. Every day the friends of the new soldiers kept coming from all parts of the county. Since they were in great numbers and swarmed over the camp, military order or discipline was next to impossible.

By September 1st recruiting was finished and all the companies had full numbers. Physical examination was then made and nearly all passed and were accepted. Then we received our uniforms and most of our equipment which included old-fashioned Enfield rifles. They were ungainly pieces having the look of old age. We carried these guns for some weeks but before going into active service they were exchanged for Springfield muskets, a much better weapon. With our other equipment we got our knapsacks in which we were supposed to place all our baggage and belongings. One of the puzzles that confronted us was how in that limited space we could carry all the good things our friends, with the kindest intentions, had given us. A list of the articles sent me would have made quite an inventory, and could I have packed them, it would have required a Samson to carry them. It was impossible to get half of them in my knapsack, so after sorting and discarding for a long time I finally sent home a larger bundle than I took with me. Even then my knapsack bulged on every side and to an old soldier would have been an object of derision. Later experience taught us how little was necessary.

On September 4th we were mustered into the service of the United States. Orders came at once for us to leave by train September 5th. The news of our sudden departure was known in every part of the county that night and in the morning thousands of the people were in Salem. I am sure the village never before or since had so great a throng of visitors. The soldiers' relations, neighbors and friends were there to give the boys their farewell word, their goodby, their well wishes and to see them off on their long journey. With many it was to be the last farewell. It was not a happy day, it was a day of sadness. Finally, late in the afternoon, we shouldered our knapsacks and marched to the train, the great crowd following us. Then there was the last handshake and kiss. The train slowly started. The people lining the track were so wrought with emotions that they found no voice to cheer. They silently waved their hands while we could see their faces filled with tears. . . .

   Late in the evening [on September 7] we left Baltimore
but not now in passenger cars. We were packed closely in
cattle cars and a hot, sweaty, hungry lot of men we were.
The only food we had was what many had left over in their
haversacks brought from Salem. It was stale enough but it
was what we had to eat or nothing. We were stowed away,
as mercilessly as though we were dumb brutes, but our patriotic ardor was running high and not many complaints
were heard. All seemed willing to suffer in the good cause.
I managed by a lot of strategy to get in a horizontal position
on the floor of the car and was weary enough to sleep well
until morning. I found on waking up we were in Annapolis
Junction. We had gone only eighteen miles during the night.
There were all sorts of absurd rumors about the conductor
of our train. He was said to be a secessionist; how in the
middle of the night he had stopped the train intending to deliver us into the hands of some guerrilla band which failed
to come through in time. The story was generally believed
and some of the boys thought the conductor ought to be
hanged; but nothing serious happened to him.
   At the junction we first saw actual soldiering, a brigade
of old soldiers was stationed there guarding the railroad.
Their little white tents were arranged neatly in streets and
made a fine appearance. As we were there early in the morning before any drilling could be done, the men were idle.
Crowds of them gathered close around our cars to see the
new recruits and to recount their hairbreadth escapes in battle. They encouraged us by saying there were some fine experiences coming to us later. A few maliciously wanted to
know if we were $140 men [men who enlisted only to col-
lect bounty money]. This, however, was taken in good part
by us and all personalities were laughed off. From Annapolis junction until we reached Washington we saw camps
scattered along the railroad, the men of whom came out to
cheer us as we passed by. Near Washington, we found that
a great camp of white tents seemed to surround the city.
   About noon our train was stopped outside the suburbs
about a mile from the depot. When we left the train we were

at once marched to the Soldiers Home for dinner. On reaching it dinner was not yet ready and the whole Regiment was
driven into and locked in an attached yard to wait until the
dinner was ready. The yard was hardly large enough to hold
the men and was the most filthy place I was ever in. It was
roughly floored and actually crawling with vermin and rats
which scampered in all directions. We were in this hole nearly an hour before "dinner" was ready and then were marched
to the dining hall and seated on rough board seats and at
rough board tables, set with tin and iron plates and cups. We
were hungry enough to eat almost anything but this dinner
was the limit. We had bread, no butter, salt pork, very salty,
and a mixture called coffee which would defy anyone to tell
by its taste whether it was tea or coffee. It must have been a
mixture of both. Well, we ate because we were faint and had
to but I can tell you it was a tough meal. It was a notorious
fact I found that the Soldiers Home in Washington was the
worst conducted institution of its kind in the whole country.
As Washington was the headquarters of the Army and everything could be had in plenty, it would seem as though the
first reception of our country's defenders should have been
at least liberal. Surely it should not be indecent. In fact it was
not liberal or even decent at this feeding shed, which has become a hiss and byword with every soldier, and has been giv-
en the name of the "Soldiers Prison.". . .

On the morning of September 16th we were ordered to
pack up, strike our tents, and be ready to move at once. Before noon we fell in and headed for the city. We marched by
the Capitol, went down Pennsylvania Avenue several blocks,
then turning south passed the Washington Monument. It was
unfinished and looked like a chimney the construction of
which had been abandoned. Soon we reached the Long
Bridge over which thousands of our soldiers had crossed.
Many of them would never return. It was more than a half-
mile long but we were only a short time reaching the other
side, there treading for the first time the sacred soil of Virginia. The ground was hard dry clay, on its good behavior.
It gave no indication of its ability in the way of mud-making

the first time we saw it. From the bridge we went in a south-easterly direction for two miles and halted near Fort Albany, one of the forts erected west of the Potomac for the defense of Washington. The place selected for our camp was on rough uneven ground, well covered with bushes and small trees. Before we could put up our tents the ground had to be grubbed and leveled. This was a hard job and it was two days before our camp was made in a satisfactory way. We were surrounded with thousands of new troops, who as soon as they reached Washington and location was provided, were sent to Arlington Heights to be drilled, disciplined and prepared for their work as soldiers. General Silas Casey was in command of this great training encampment. He was an old officer, a rigid disciplinarian, and was expected to give these new regiments a thorough training so that after a few weeks they could be assigned to active service at the front. When this was done the new regiments would usually be sandwiched between older ones that had seen service.

Near us was a regiment from Massachusetts that had been well drilled by a competent Colonel. While we were at Arlington they received orders to go to the front. Before they started they were visited by President Lincoln, Secretary William H. Seward and the two Massachusetts Senators, Charles Sumner and Henry Wilson. A great crowd of soldiers from the surrounding regiments gathered around the carriage of the visitors and after cheering called on the President for a speech. He arose from his seat and spoke for five or ten minutes. He was serious and tried to impress upon the soldiers the responsibility that rested on them, saying that it would be their efforts alone that would save the country. He looked thin and worn and one could see that he was troubled and anxious. He remained some time after he spoke so many of us had an opportunity to take his hand and have a word of greeting. . . .

At this camp we were kept busy drilling. There was a large parade ground not far south of us where regimental and brigade drills were held. General Casey conducted the brigade movements which were mostly in changing front.

These were tiresome when we happened to be on the extreme flank and had to make the long swing to get into line. While there we had one review, in which twenty regiments took part. As they were all new regiments, with full ranks and bright new uniforms, we made a fine show. But, our marching was hardly up to standard. There was also picket duty on a line some two miles from the camp. This was not dangerous, as the enemy was no nearer than twenty miles, but it did give training. All were anxious to go on the picket line as it gave us a chance to visit some of the farmhouses located there where we could purchase a meal. This food seemed wonderfully good compared with our rations. While in Arlington I think we suffered from real hunger as much as we did at any time during our service; not that we did not have plenty of army food of excellent quality, but we had not yet reached the point where we could appreciate and eat the "stuff" as the boys called it. A certain length of time was required to bring us to the starvation point and we found it at this camp. When we had taken to the army ration we had no further trouble, for it was sufficient when we could get it. At Arlington the pie bakers were legion and it was amusing to see the boys line up to buy them as they were baked. They were so hungry they would stand in line for hours to get a pie which cost 25 cents. But it was at this camp that we passed through the childlike period of soldiering and became reconciled to our food and other conditions that we had to face in the service.

Our training period in the camp at Arlington lasted about two weeks. The weather was fine, we were becoming acclimated and the health of the men was excellent. Every day we learned something, not alone military evolutions. We were learning by experience how to care for ourselves and how better to overcome the conditions we had to contend with, which we first thought almost unbearable and unnecessary. We were now becoming reconciled to discipline and commenced to realize that we were only being fitted for the work before us.

The morning of September 29th we struck our tents,

packed our knapsacks and by midday were ready to move. About three in the afternoon we started in the direction of Washington, crossing the Long Bridge at four. This was to be the last time we crossed the bridge until we crossed it to take part in the Grand Review of Sherman's Army three years later. Then there were less than half of those with us on September 29th. The others had died in action or from disease, or had left the service because of wounds or sickness.

After crossing the bridge we marched to the railroad station to take a train to some place unknown to us. That night we slept on the sidewalk as the train was not ready until seven the next morning. We left the city on flat cars, traveling slowly. There were many trains on the road and we spent much of our time on sidings. Just as night came we reached Frederick, Maryland. We stopped before entering the town and filed into the meadows where we were to spend the night. When we were dismissed we dropped to the ground where most convenient and spread our blankets for bed. It had been a hard day for us, crowded as we were on flat cars with no seats.

There had been no way to prepare meals so all we had to eat after leaving Arlington had been the hardtack that we had in our haversacks. Our company cooks made us some coffee which we drank with what was left of our hardtack. I felt as hungry as if I had not eaten for I had not yet reached the soldierly perfection when two or three pieces of hardtack and coffee could be made to satisfy my hunger. We remained two days at Frederick, where we learned that we were soon to join the Army of the Potomac in the vicinity of Harpers Ferry.

The Army was expected to advance soon. October 4th, we took the train again and went to some station near Harpers Ferry. From there we marched two or three miles up beautiful Pleasant Valley and camped some three miles from the Ferry. We were to remain here until assigned to some Division of the Army. We would then enter active service after being in the Army only one month. Thus early and practically untrained we were at the front waiting orders for active field duty.

Meeting the Rebs at Fair Oaks

Charles Harvey Brewster

The first year of the war passed calmly enough—almost too calmly for the eager soldiers who had volunteered for the Union. But in the spring of 1862, the fighting began to grow hot during the Peninsula campaign, which was General McLellan's attempt to sail around the Confederate defenses and make a direct attack on the Confederate capital at Richmond.

Both sides were eager for the fight, and the spirit displayed by Confederate and Union volunteers played a big part in turning this campaign into a long, complex, and drawn-out stalemate. Massachusetts infantryman Charles Harvey Brewster describes his encounter with death and battle at Fair Oaks, an early Peninsula fight, in this eloquent letter home.

6 miles from Richmond Va
Monday June 2nd 1862

Dear Mother
I presume this letter will find you most anxiously expecting a letter from me. I am sitting in the hot sun and can write you but a few lines.

Last Saturday afternoon as we were lying quietly in camp the guns began to crack just in front. the fire grew hotter + hotter and in just a few moments the order came for us to fall in which we did and immediately moved forward in line of battle. We were in this direction for about 50 yards and

Charles Harvey Brewster, letter to his mother, June 2, 1862.

then moved to the left, and took position in some rifle pits, immediately behind Gen Casey's Divisions camp, and Oh Mother, I cannot begin to give you any idea of the terrific storm of bullets, shot + shell, that poured over us as we lay behind those pits. we could not get into them for they were full to brim of water, but we lay right behind them in the mud. After half an hour of this, the firing ceased and we were ordered forward behind some fallen woods, which had been cut down, and had just got our line formed, when in the woods at our left, and rear appeared the Rebels. Co G was the left Co and Co C came next and I never shall forget the moment when I turned and saw them through a small opening hardly three rods from me, taking aim at us almost directly behind our backs. It was but an instant and there was a roar, and a perfect rain of bullets came pouring into us. I felt the wind of them on my face and men fell dead + wounded on every side. The line was hardly formed and of course it was immediately broken.

I tried my best to make a face to the rear toward them, and to add to the general confusion it was a matter of great doubt whether they were rebels, or our own men, and we restrained half our fire in that account. The order was immediately given to fall back and form some more fallen brush just behind us, but it was impossible, everything was in confusion and we could not see 3 rods from us in any direction so the order was given to rally on the camp, which we did. Capt Parsons was wounded at the first volley, though I did not know it at the time nor until we formed in front of the camp again, which we did as quick as possible, though with greatly diminished numbers, and were immediately ordered to the left again into the rifle pits where we were before, and here we crossed the field again in a perfect torrent of shot + shell and every other missile of destruction. We lay here for some time again and here we had two or three more wounded.

"The Hottest Fire I Was In"

Pretty soon the firing broke out very hot on the right and we were ordered across the field again to the right. Across we went and formed behind a low ridge and faced them, and fought our best, but they turned us again on our right and left, where we had no support. We fell back over another ridge, right in our camp and here we faced them again but twas a hopeless task "a forlorn hope" then Col Briggs fell and was taken up and carried to rear entreating and commanding his bearers to stop, and put him down. He would not leave the field, but they kept on. What few there were of us rallied round the colors and retreated through a strip of woods in which was our camp, but we could not stop to take anything with us as the foe were right on our heels and pouring in a perfect storm of bullets. As we came out in an open field in the rear of this woods we found the remnant of a regiment, the 93rd NY or Pa, I do not know which, NY I think, though they hailed us to form on thier left and go in with them and make one more effort. Capt Miller of Co H (Shelbourne Falls) was in command of the shattered wreck of the once glorious 10th, and there was one other Capt, Smart of N Adams. We hesitated a moment for we knew it was useless, but Massachusetts men were not to have it said that they refused when anybody else made a stand, so we went in again.

Forming lines, back we went, urged on by Gen Heinztleman, Keyes, + Devens, the latter on foot with a shattered leg. I had of Co Cs being in command 3 Sergts, Bishop, Nims, + Munyan 2 Corporals Loomis + Moody, and 4 or 5 privates which was all the company I had, but they were true grit and knew not fear, and this little remnent of two Regts went in to those woods again, and met the host of the enemy, and held them at bay for a short time. It was the hottest fire I was in during the day. Co H suffered terribly here, losing thier 2nd Lieut Leland and four sergts. They were on the left of the line and in the road that went through the woods, consequently the most exposed. The rest of us being partly protected by the woods. Cousin George was in command of Co F also in this last tug and had about the same number that I did. His Capt would not go in the last time. *I guess that George and I have kept the old Brewster blood in good repute,* at any rate we did not shirk from duty, until Gen Devens himself told us to fall back behind the other line of rifle pits. I have written you about them I put a letter of twenty pages which I have been writing from day to day while the departure of the mail was prohibited, but I expect it is in the hands of the Rebels as I cannot learn certainly but the general impression seems to be that the mail was not sent that day before the battle, if so I hope it will put thier eyes out when they read it. I have lost everything that I had in camp, except what I had on my back namely my clothes and my sword and pistol, and so have all the Co. My Haversack, Field Glass, Knapsack, Blankets, Rubber O Coat, and the pretty cap Mary sent me last, are all gone to the benefit of the occursed Rebels. What I lost there cost me over thirty dollars, fortunately my valise containing my sash, clothes and pictures of Matt and Mary was back with the team behind the Chickahominy.

Sensible to the Last

We had but 7 Companies in the fight the other 3 were on Picket. Our loss in the regiment is 27 killed, 84 wounded and 14 missing, total 125, or one out of four of the strength engaged. In Co C, we have lost in killed, wounded and missing, 21. Capt Parsons will be home before this reaches you. I did not see him from the time we went into the battle when he was wounded until just as the cars having him on board left yesterday I sent word by him to make it his first duty to tell you that I was safe. Lieut Wetherill is in Hospital sick, and although I aught to be, I cannot leave the co, as I have to make requisitions for a complete fitout for the co and everything else in my hands. Sergt Braman was killed by a Cannon shot or shell when we fell back the second time. He had been wounded in the leg, but was able to go until the shell or shot took his shoulder and arm completely off. He was brought to the rear and lived until about 8 o'clock that evening. He did his duty and died a hero. He was sensible to the last. He is buried in a garden close by here and in the best order that could possibly be done under the circumstances. I did not see him after that fight and did not know of his death until morning. Private Putnam, another of our dead, is another hero. He died while being brought out on a stretcher. His last words were, "Tell Capt Parsons I died a soldier". He was the man I have written you about once or

Looking at the Enemy

In Embattled Courage: The Experience of Combat in the Civil War, *Gerald F. Linderman summarizes the early view of enemy soldiers commonly taken by the troops of the North.*

At the outbreak of the war ferocity characterized each side's image of the other. Southerners denied that those who confronted them were American soldiers. No, the Union Army was an assemblage of immigrants, of European marauders, a "hireling host," "the refuse of the earth." By their nature such people would invade and ravage other people's land. From the Northern side, the enemy appeared less distant but just as deplorable: Southerners were traitors. Writing to his brother Henry on the eve of his entry into the Union army, Charles Francis Adams, Jr., decided that he "could fight with a will and in earnest" against the rebels. "They are traitors, they war for a lie, they are the enemies of morals, of government, and of man. In them, we fight against a great wrong." Occasionally, such images persisted to color actual observations of the enemy. A Vermonter watched Confederate troops of Jackson's command cross a pontoon bridge following their capture of Harper's Ferry in the early autumn of 1862: "They were silent as ghosts; ruthless and rushing in their speed; ragged, earth colored, dishevelled and devilish, as tho' they were keen on the scent of the hot blood that was already streaming up from the opening struggle at [the Battle of] Antietam, and thirsting for it."

Gerald F. Linderman, *Embattled Courage: The Experience of Combat in the Civil War.* New York: The Free Press, 1987.

twice as sharing his blanket with me etc. etc. A generous open hearted, whole souled soldier of the Union, besides him and Sergt Braman, it is almost positively known that Francis W. White and Perry N. Coleman are dead, but there is a bare possibility that they are wounded and prisoners.

Yesterday Sunday, they had another and it is said a harder fight on our right, and tis said they piled up the Rebels like cord wood I suppose we have the Rebels cornered between Richmond and the Chickahominy and that these battles are thier last desparate struggles. We are now lying behind a long line of rifle pits with an open field of 50 acres or more in front, and all the Rebels in Dixie cannot drive us from here. I have slept under a Rubber Blanket two nights by favor of the boys, and am liable to sleep without anything for some nights to come. I don't know whether Capt W is going to get well enough to take command or not but I hope he will for if there was any other officer here with our co I should go somewhere. I have been sick for three weeks and yesterday when I went into the fight it seemed as though I should not be able to stand a half an hour but I went through hard labor enough to kill a man if it were not for the excitement, but still now that it is over it seems as if I could not keep around. I was down at the hospital and saw Lieut Wetherill yesterday afternoon, and he said he should be up this morning but it is noon and he has not appeared I cannot succeed in giving you any idea of the battle, but I know this much that I had no possible hope of coming out alive, and I thought it all over how terribly you would feel and all that, but I came out without a scratch. I look back upon it and I cannot think how it can be. It does not seem as though any man that had been there could come out unhurt.

Capt Smart of Co B (No Adams) is killed. He was killed in the last struggle last night. Capt Day of Co G (Greenfield) is killed. He was killed in the second stand we made. I presume this must seem like a very confused account but I cannot make it plainer until I can tell you by word of mouth about it. There are so many incidents crowding my head, that I cannot write clearly at all and even when I sleep, the minute I get into a doze I hear the whistling of the shells and the shouts and groans, and to sum it up in two words it is *horrible.*

Cal K was sick and did not go into the fight though the fight came to him. He and Johnnie Cook are all safe and sound. Wm Mather was shot through both legs. Wm M Kingsley (Geo Kingsley's son) was shot through both legs and a number of others whom you would not know were very severely wounded and we have a dozen men that were hit but not hurt who were not included in the list of the casualties. You must tell Cals folks and Johnnies all about them or show them this letter and don't fail to write me often and let us hope this horrible work will be over soon. We are under marching orders, that is to be ready at a moments notice all the time and may have to go at any time. There is fighting all around us today as it sounds like it, for we hear cannon in every direction. We had two alarms and stood to arms in the night last night, and 3 o'clock PM is the latest we sleep mornings now. I wish the scoundrels would once show themselves on this open field. We would give them all they ask for and more too in the way of reception. The great trouble is they have got us in this miserable country, half swamp and they know every inch, and we know nothing about it. However if the right wing gets behind them we shall have them, dead or alive. We have taken lots of prisoners. They are coming in constantly. In the fight on the right yesterday, they took 350 including a Brigadere Gen, several Cols and several Lieut Cols. It is so hot I cannot write any more. Give my love all and pray for the end of this war, with much love Your aff son

Charlie.

Battling the Confederate Army of Virginia

Lorenzo Barnhart

The normal period of enlistment for Union soldiers was three full years, or until the end of the war (whichever came first). After their initial training, infantry units such as the 110th Ohio Volunteers were often hurried to the front to fill sudden gaps caused by battlefield losses that weakened, and sometimes destroyed, older regiments. The units remained active as long as possible; after forming up at Camp Piqua, Ohio, the 110th Ohio saw action in twenty-one separate battles.

In these memoirs, Private Lorenzo D. Barnhart expresses great pride in the role played by his unit in the days just before the battle of Gettysburg in the summer of 1863. The Ohio volunteers held up the entire Confederate army of Virginia for three days at Winchester, Virginia, before moving onto Harpers Ferry, West Virginia, and Gettysburg, Pennsylvania.

Everything was quiet until Saturday the 13th day of June, 1863. The weather was fine and balmy we wished we were at home to help the farmers plant corn. Something else turned up our vidette [mounted sentries] were fired on, also our pickets [advanced infantry line] by the Confederates. We did not know what force was coming against us out on the Winchester and Strawsburg Pike. We were ready for them our pickets engaged them I was on the picket line myself it was

Reprinted from "Reminiscences of Lorenzo D. Barnhart, Company 3, 110th Ohio Volunteers."

the first engagement we were in and we seen how they fought. We matched them at there own game, they kept hid behind Cedar and Pine bushes and field rock and stumps. They were called the Mississippi and Louisiana Tigers, we did not know until afterwards what force we were fighting. There were only 7 thousand of us and about 70 or 80 thousand of them against us. We fought them all the same although our force only made a skirmish line but we held them out side on the 12th. On Saturday, the 13th, they pushed us in our last resort. At first we met them out about 1 mile from our center we fought and retreated towards our center. We held them stubbornly and disputed every inch of ground. They were fighting us with a heavy skirmish line at once they charged onto us with a whole regiment on our light skirmish line we gave them a volley from our skirmish line then retreated toward our center. They pressed on they now used cannons and shot something at us we thought it was pieces of railroad iron. It screamed and whizzed over our heads and made a deathly noise some of these missiles went over our heads and some lit on the ground we could hear them thump.

"Like Turtles Drop Off a Log"

Now on Sunday, the 14th, in the afternoon my company B. of the 110th was sent to guard a battery of canons they were behind earth works Co. B was also behind rifle pits for us to fight behind and keep the enemy from capturing our guns. Every thing was quiet on Sunday the 14th, the boys were laying on the parapets in the sun. We came to the conclusion the confederates had all went to Church to get religion but they were only fixing to kill all of us. There was a pine mountain off about a 1/4 of a mile, all at once here came a showere of shot and shell the boys tumbled off the parapets behind them like turtles drop off a log into the water the pine mountain fairly blazed with canon they sent showers of shot and shell at us we could not reach them with our small rifles it seemed they let loose about 50 or 60 canons. Could do nothing to them they shot our little guns wheels off and upset them then they ceased fireing off the pine mountain and our officers gave us orders to fix bayonets and our guns loaded and watch over the field in front of us so we could see the Confederate infantry come out of the brush out of the raviene. We were also ordered to have our guns loaded and bayonets fixed we would not get to shoot only one shot then use our bayonets and club with our guns. They came in dress order we gave them a volley low down in their legs and they drop out of ranks. We made large gaps on their lines but they did not stop for that they closed ranks shoulder to shoulder they had been in such scrapes before. They gave us a volley then came unto us with bayonets and a yell like indians we used our gun stocks to them the front and to the rear we clubbed with them a while but to no use. We hurt some of them but what could 80 soldiers do to 70 or 80 thousand. They overpowered us but we made it hot for them for a moment it was clubbing with the butts of guns and thrusting the bayonet at and through each other. For a moment it look like Hell. What could Co. B do to them, I thought, all would get killed if we did not surrender.

We did not surrender, we just quit and every man for himself. I seen my chance to get in a ravine close by and follow it I did and then had to cross a level piece of ground to get to our last resort and fort. While crossing this I was in plain view of them they seen me get away they sent the shot after me but I would not halt. I went ahead towards the fort with three bullets plowing the ground around my feet. I looked to be hit any moment but I ran the gauntlet all safe, but my clothes was pierced with bullets but my skin was not cut. I did not want to serve my time in a Confederate prison that is why I undertook to run the gauntlet. As I did the howitzers and canon in the last fort shot over my head to keep them back so they would not come across to our last fort. That evening they held them from advancing onto us that evening I laid down on the ground close to the last fort. Night came and they were afraid to advance any farther that night General Milroy called a council of his colonels and told them they would either surrender in the morning or fight till the last man was killed or cut there lines and make our escape.

The colonels all voted to cut our way out that night. I was

awakened about one or two o'clock that night to go down to the Martinsburg Pike and fall in line and not to speak above a whisper I went and there was a battalion representatives of all the regiments around Winchester, Va. I went in line with them and expected there would something to be done now. The command was given in a whisper—"Forward March"— we went east on the pike, then north through a brushy new ground, then east again into a woods. In there were the Confederate pickets, we choke them off so they could not give the alarm, then we went through their lines. When we got out we turned to the right outside of their lines marched across the Martinsburgh Pike toward Harper's Ferry outside of their lines towards a place called Stevenson's Station. Then we halted and Colonel J. Warren Keifer of the 110th O.V.I. [Ohio Volunteer Infantry] asked permission of General Milroy if he might charge in those woods on the Confederates. Milroy said yes you may Colonel it will keep the gap open for more of the boys to get out. Col. Keifer gave the command "Attention—110th-122nd-116th-123rd-O.V.I. prepare for a charge" then he pointed in the woods. Forward we went in with a double quick when we got close enough we gave them a volley of minnie balls [rifle bullets] for their breakfast. They were dumbfounded for a while they did not know what it meant from the outside of their lines, they leveled there artillery and musketry onto us then the limbs of the trees came down on us. When our ammunition was exhausted we then retreated out of the woods in an open field where General Milroy was waiting for us to give us the final command. He pointed towards Harper's Ferry and said every man find your way through to Harper's Ferry he said do not take the pike, the pike is patroled by the enemy and you will be captured.

Fighting at Gettysburg

About 3000 got out through the gap the balance were captured with our hospitals and Sibley tents with all our things except our guns and cartridge boxes and belt. What got out represented all the regiments who were at Winchester. I took the course pointed out by General Milroy but about one half of the boys did not go the way they were showen. They went straight east ahead of the Confederate army the way it was going and did get to Harper's Ferry but went to Philadelphia and Harrisburg, Pa. and they missed the battle of Gettysburg, Pa. The battalion I was in helped to evacuate Maryland Heights. We loaded all the government property on a canal boat and took them down to Georgetown, Washington D.C. There, we left them and went aboard cars and was sent to Baltimore, Md. from there to Gettysburg, Pa. There we represented our regiment in that great battle. We went in the 3rd Army Corps of the Potomac commanded by General Meade. We did not get the credit we should had fighting the Confederate army so hard at Winchester and detaining them so long. We saved the people of Pa. and N.Y. many millions of dollars by holding them 3 days at Winchester, Va. Joe Hooker had command of the Army of the Potomac and it had been fighting at Fredericksburg and at Marye's Heights near Fredericksburg. Here General R.E. Lee's Confederate army sneaked away from the front of Joe Hooker and came down the Shenandoah Valley and surrounded our 7 thousand at Winchester Va.

Now look at the map where Fredericksburg and Winchester is and General Joe Hooker didn't know what R.E. Lee's intention was until he had us surounded at Winchester and we did not know what number of force was against us there. But we fought and found out it was the whole Confederate Army of Nothern Virginia about 70 or 80 thousand strong against 7 thousand of us. We held them for 3 days and made it pretty hot for them until Joe Hooker came up and met them at Gettysburg Pa. Along the way Hooker was relieved from the command and General Meade was put in command of the army. He fought the battle of Gettysburg and commanded the Army of the Potomac until the surender at Appomattox C.H. [courthouse] Va. on the 9th day of April, 1865. We followed Lee's army from Gettysburg across the Potomac River into his own state Virginia and fought him all summer between Washington and the Rapidan River in the fall of 1863 and 1864.

Riding and Raiding in Virginia

Samuel E. Cormany

Soon after marrying Rachel Bowman, Samuel Cormany settled down to raise his family in the Grand River Valley of Canada, his wife's birthplace. But in the summer of 1862, news of the Civil War and the Union's desperate need for soldiers prompted him to return to Pennsylvania, where he settled his young family in the Cumberland valley. Cormany volunteered and was mustered into the 16th Pennsylvania Cavalry, a volunteer regiment that was to see action in most of the eastern campaigns right up to the final battle at Appomattox in the spring of 1865.

To a volunteer like Samuel Cormany, the life of a Union cavalryman may have appeared exciting and purposeful. But the pursuit of Confederate units after the Battle of Gettysburg, and the fighting at the Battle of Shepherdstown, in West Virginia, described in these diary entries, left him exhausted and apprehensive. Although they were fast-moving and well-armed, cavalry units were vulnerable to massed infantry, artillery, and sharpshooters, and casualties during hit-and-run raids as well as set battles were high. Despite the fact that the Union was in pursuit and the Confederate armies were on the defensive, the 16th Pennsylvania found some rough going at Shepherdstown.

July 7, 1863 Tuesday. Oh! how sweet to love and be loved. I kissed my Darlings Good-bye, and at 7 A.M.

Excerpted from Samuel Cormany's diary entries for July 7 to July 21, 1863.

started back to join my Regiment at Greenwood.

Now that I have again seen my dearest ones of Earth, have loved and caressed them profusely, soldiering seems almost a new thing again—and altogether desirable—since country, home, and dear ones must be defended.

Reached the Regiment about 9 A.M. Corp Metz had done the nice thing—and he and I took our dinners at Fayetteville.

In the P.M. we marched on through Funkstown—En route 6 Rebs gave themselves up—Corp Metz & I took charge of them—We encamped near Quincy— . . .

July 10, 1863 Friday. Hot—Lay in field roasting all day P.M. Moved camp a few 100 yrds. 13 of our Alexandria Boys joined us with new horses—and 3 absent without leave showed up—They had been visiting—

July 11, 1863 Saturday. NEWS Vicksburg [Mississippi] has fallen [to Union forces under General Ulysses S. Grant]. A.M. I wrote for Pet—

P.M. Took up line of March. Passed where some of our advance had a little brush yesterday—Eve Camp near Boonesboro.

July 12, 1863 Sunday. Not much going on save "Camp rumors"—Rained furiously—Some of the Boys almost swam away. . . .

July 15, 1863 Wednesday. Started out early to Halltown, rested awhile—had considerable skirmishing and charging all the way to Shepherdstown—we made a tremendous dash into town, surprising and capturing quite a number of Rebs—also—some invalids. There were some 30 fighting fellows and 80 invalids taken—also some provisions—Tents, &c.

I had a fine chat with some of the rebel Ladies—I do admire their pluck—what a pity their minds didn't run in a different Channel—a better channel. So the efforts of such animated feelings would not be so hopelessly wasted on a waning cause tottering on its last legs—We followed the retreating [Confederates] closely some 8 miles—I was in extreme advance in charge of a section of our best men—We fired on them frequently—i.e., their rear and so kept them

well closed up—Evening we encamped near Mrs. Kroates—
I got a fine supper.

July 16, 1863 Thursday. Has cleared—I got a fine breakfast at Mrs Kroates. Mr. K. is gone to Penna.—We changed
camp at 10 A.M. ½ mile. Dined at Mrs. K's—I have been
kind-o-guarding her home, seeing he is loyal and is away—

About noon, skirmishing commences. Soon our Regt was
dismounted and in front advancing across open field—
firing at will—enemy was in a woods—long range—Sharp
shooting ¼ to ½ mile—I with several, along our line, crept
far out front behind stumps and rocks and picked the enemy
sharpshooters out of trees. Soon our whole line was hotly
engaged—Enemy advancing out of the woods—but we held
our line, checking them. Soon we were under the hotest
cross-fire we ever were in—and had to fall back on line with
an old house and stone fence and stone piles—my buddy—
was shot through the breast at my left and dropping said,
"Oh I am shot—tell my Mother." and he was hushed. bullits
passed close to my head. I dodged behind a stone pile and
fired at the man who had shot Buddy—Raising his head
above the stone fence protecting him. His bullet whizzed
close to my right ear—I made a port hole by pushing up two

*A sharpshooter lies dead at Gettysburg after enemy forces spotted him in the
trees.*

stones and one to cap the space and putting my carbine through my head was shielded. After this the rocks were hit once—My gun was ready, and soon his head came up and he craned his neck to find me—Then my gun went off— and—I don't know—But he didn't show up to shoot again. Soon I found the men to my right and left were falling back and I was compelled to do so too. As I retreated toward the Boys, directly two rebs appeared, less than 100 yds to my right—having just emerged from some bushes and weeds— and had the drop on me. Instead of throwing up my arms to surrender—I banged away. One of them dropped his gun. The other fired wild—I fired again on the run—a small vol- ley followed me—but I reached the fence where our line was, and so was safe(?) again—The rebel line was coming across the same ground—a daring Flag bearer was away front. Came within 100 yds of us—I said "Boys drop that Rebel Flag" We fired—The flag fell. Another reb picked it up—another little volley and it dropped again—another picked it up, and stepped behind a lone tree—held it out, i.e., The flagpole resting on the ground—The arm extend- ing from the tree—held the pole erect. Again our little group fired "for that arm" and the flag fell—all this while to the right and left of me and my Bunch—the regiment was fir- ing from this fence—and the enemy was moving rather cau- tiously and slowly but was now very close—a little lull— BOOM! a shell drops within 20 or 30 feet of us. Explodes throwing ground over us—making an excavation large enough to roll a horse in out of sight—a piece of that shell hit my right arm between the shoulder and elbow. My first thought was "There goes my right arm"—But it was not gone—though badly bruised—

Here came the hotest time yet. Shells—Grape [grapeshot shells] in front—and infantry crossfire—and a charge— Infantry against dismounted Cavalry—

Nine pieces of artillery were in play—Our Boys stood to the stone fence—A while I carried ammunition—as my arm was too sore to allow my using my carbine—In this I be- came a fine (?) target for sharpshooters—

We held our part of the line though they several times charged as close to our fence as 50 to 100 yards or nearer—at such times our men used their Revolvers and forced them to fall back and reform—

Kindly darkness came on so we could only fire at their fire—But we held our line against every effort they made—Their firing becoming less and less frequent. About 10 P.M. they ceased firing. Later we fired a few shots. There was no response, so we sent out a few scouts and found they had withdrawn and about 11 ock [o'clock] orders came for us to return to our horses—and fall back to Boliver Heights and encamp—Picket line had been established—So we gave ourselves to seeking rest and comfort—amidst rain and rain and rain. Of course, we all were very much exhausted.

The tension was fearful, for we well knew we were fighting against fearful odds—

July 17, 1863 Friday. After Battle of Shephardstown. Boliver Heights I feel quite unwell—used up—We lay 'round resting most of day—My arm & shoulder very bruised, and lame, from a hit by a piece of rebel shell, yesterday, and the jar from so much carbine shooting—

Evening we drew some clothing for our comfort &c.

Read and meditated some The Lord is SO GOOD to have spared me through another such terrific battle.

July 18, 1863 Saturday. Cleared up I am very stiff in my right arm and shoulder—But have no difficulty in performing full duty.

I took a good bath in the Shenandoah River—made me feel lots better—P.M. Captain Snyder and I rode Harpers Ferry Hospital—Sergt Harrison wounded in right knee—rests easy—Poor Will Goodman and Corp'l S.A. Rorabough mortally wounded—both died soon after being taken off the field—

July 19, 1863 Sunday. Fine day—Rested—My arm quite sore to the touch—and somewhat stiff—Eve we left camp, crossed the Shenandoah on Bridge—went down along the River—some grand-romantic scenery—at 10 P.M. we put up at Lovettsville—

July 20, 1863 Monday. This morning Capt Snyder announced that "for conspicuous bravery during the battle at Shepherdstown—four days ago—Sam'l E. Cormany has been promoted to Sergeant and Jerome Coble to Corporal and the Company is hereby ordered to recognize them as such at all times"—

We took up line of March early, via Leesburg—Folks look awfully surly at us as we pass—we can see our unwelcomeness—and no wonder! We defeated Lee at Gettysburg and drove his Army back to Virginnia, and only last Thursday we thoroughly defeated a large force of them at Shephardstown, and induced them to fall back here in Virginnia, and here we are! A column of Triumphant Fellows, moving along their streets, and their "Boasters" still on the retreat.— Evening we put up at a Mill on Goose Creek—I am well but suffer some from my bruised arm—

July 21, 1863 Tuesday. Marched all day—Went via Centerville. Great fortifications here. Went on across Bull Run and bivouaced—Put out two squadrons on picket duty towards Evening—Endless patches of Blackberries, and we did up quantities of the choicest berries—both Evening and morning—

Chapter 3

In the Officer's Tent

Chapter Preface

At the start of the war, the Confederacy enjoyed a crucial advantage in its officer corps. Three of the most important generals of the South—Robert E. Lee, James Longstreet, and "Stonewall" Jackson—were experienced and talented officers. On the Union side, President Lincoln began a frustrating search for capable military leaders through a process of trial and error.

Union officers were quickly replaced upon achieving bad results in battle, while the endless political maneuvering in Washington played an important part in many crucial promotions and demotions. After the Union's defeat at Bull Run on July 21, 1861, Lincoln replaced the commander of the Army of the Potomac, General Irvin McDowell, with General George B. McClellan, who would later be replaced by General Ambrose Burnside, who in turn was replaced by General Joseph Hooker. In the meantime, there was considerable grumbling among junior officers over the actions of their superiors, and an uneven performance on the part of company commanders, who in many volunteer units had gained their positions by a popular vote among their men.

Lincoln knew that simply occupying enemy territory would not be sufficient to win the war; instead, the opposing armies had to be defeated. For this he would need officers of skill and experience, and they were in short supply in the months after the defeat at Bull Run. Indeed, several of the officers who would lead the Union army to victory—among them William T. Sherman, Philip Sheridan, and Ulysses S. Grant—were civilians when the war began.

Grant Takes Command in Missouri

Ulysses S. Grant

The poor performance and hesitation of the Union generals at the start of the war exasperated President Lincoln. By 1862 the government was searching for new leaders, and presenting a time of opportunity for men with courage and cunning. Ulysses S. Grant, a veteran of the war with Mexico, had returned to civilian life in Illinois only to fail at farming as well as in business. He heartily welcomed his commission as a brigadier general in the Union army.

Grant's first orders were to march his old regiment, the 21st Illinois, into southern Missouri and capture a Confederate position. Still new to generalship, Grant found the volunteer regiments he led as uncertain and confused as he was. However, through good intelligence, he managed to prevent the Confederate army from occupying strategic towns.

I had not been in Mexico many weeks when, reading a St. Louis paper, I found the President had asked the Illinois delegation in Congress to recommend some citizens of the State for the position of brigadier-general, and that they had unanimously, recommended me as first on a list of seven. I was very much surprised because, as I have said, my acquaintance with the Congressmen was very limited and I did not know of anything I had done to inspire such confidence.

Excerpted from *Personal Memoirs of U.S. Grant*, by Ulysses S. Grant (New York: Webster, 1885).

The papers of the next day announced that my name, with three others, had been sent to the Senate, and a few days after our confirmation was announced. . . .

Questioning Authority

Shortly after my promotion I was ordered to Ironton, Missouri, to command a district in that part of the State, and took the 21st Illinois, my old regiment, with me. Several other regiments, were ordered to the same destination about the same time. Ironton is on the Iron Mountain railroad, about seventy miles south of St. Louis, and situated among hills rising almost to the dignity of mountains. When I reached there, about the 8th of August, Colonel B. Gratz Brown—afterwards Governor of Missouri and in 1872 Vice-Presidential candidate—was in command. Some of his troops were ninety days' men [troops whose tour of duty was 90 days] and their time had expired some time before. The men had no clothing but what they had volunteered in, and much of this was so worn that it would hardly stay on. General Hardee—the author of the tactics I did not study— was at Greenville, some twenty-five miles further south, it was said, with five thousand Confederate troops. Under these circumstances Colonel Brown's command was very much demoralized. A squadron of cavalry could have ridden into the valley and captured the entire force. Brown himself was gladder to see me on that occasion than he ever has been since. I relieved him and sent all his men home, within a day or two, to be mustered out of service.

Within ten days after reaching Ironton I was prepared to take the offensive against the enemy at Greenville. I sent a column east out of the valley we were in, with orders to swing around to the south and west and come into the Greenville road ten miles south of Ironton. Another column marched on the direct road and went into camp at the point designated for the two columns to meet. I was to ride out the next morning and take personal command of the movement. My experience against Harris, in northern Missouri, had inspired me with confidence. But when the evening train came in, it brought General B. M. Prentiss with orders to take command of the district. His orders did not relieve me, but I knew that by law I was senior, and at that time even the President did not have the authority to assign a junior to command a senior of the same grade. I therefore gave General Prentiss the situation of the troops and the general condition of affairs, and started for St. Louis the same day. The movement against the rebels at Greenville went no further.

Restoring Order

From St. Louis I was ordered to Jefferson City, the capital of the State, to take command. General Stirling Price, of the Confederate army, was thought to be threatening the capital, Lexington, Chillicothe and other comparatively large towns in the central part of Missouri. I found a good many troops in Jefferson City, but in the greatest confusion, and no one person knew where they all were. Colonel Mulligan, a gallant man, was in command, but he had not been educated as yet to his new profession and did not know how to maintain discipline. I found that volunteers had obtained permission from the department commander, or claimed they had, to raise, some of them, regiments; some battalions; some companies—the officers to be commissioned according to the number of men they brought into the service. There were recruiting stations all over town, with notices, rudely lettered on boards over the doors, announcing the arm of service and length of time for which recruits at that station would be received. The law required all volunteers to serve for three years or the war. But in Jefferson City in August, 1861, they were recruited for different periods and on different conditions; some were enlisted for six months, some for a year, some without any condition as to where they were to serve, others were not to be sent out of the State. The recruits were principally men from regiments stationed there and already in the service, bound for three years if the war lasted that long.

The city was filled with Union fugitives who had been driven by guerrilla bands to take refuge with the National troops. They were in a deplorable condition and must have starved but for the support the government gave them. They had generally made their escape with a team or two, sometimes a yoke of oxen with a mule or a horse in the lead. A little bedding besides their clothing and some food had been thrown into the wagon. All else of their worldly goods were abandoned and appropriated by their former neighbors; for the Union man in Missouri who staid at home during the rebellion, if he was not immediately under the protection of the National troops, was at perpetual war with his neighbors. I stopped the recruiting service, and disposed the troops

Grant's Victory Plan

By 1864, President Lincoln had grown exasperated with his timid and ineffective generals. He placed Ulysses S. Grant in charge of the entire Union army, explaining to skeptical aides that "I can't spare this man; he fights." Although he presented an unimpressive appearance, Grant proved to be the best military strategist of the war. In his book A Short History of the Civil War, *James L. Stokesbury explains Grant's grand design for bringing the Union its final victory.*

After his quick visit [to Washington in 1864], Grant returned to the west to bring about a command reorganization there, and to mature his plans for the campaign that would soon open. Sherman was now to command the Military Division of the Mississippi; he and Grant had already reached substantial understanding on how the war should be conducted from this stage on. There has been some discussion among historians as to who developed what plan when, but the two principals never argued about it; they enjoyed a very real synchronicity of minds, and had a clear picture of what they wanted to do.

Thus when Grant returned to Washington at the end of the month, and discussed his situation with President Lincoln, he had already worked out his main line of advance. The president had himself produced a plan, for a waterborne end-run around Lee's army, and he propounded it with great de-

about the outskirts of the city so as to guard all approaches. Order was soon restored. . . .

Maneuvers in Kentucky

The day after I assumed command [of volunteer regiments] at Cairo [Illinois] a man came to me who said he was a scout of General [John C.] Fremont. He reported that he had just come from Columbus, a point on the Mississippi twenty miles below on the Kentucky side, and that troops had started from there, or were about to start, to seize Paducah, at the mouth of the Tennessee. There was no time for delay; I re-

---

tail and equal diffidence. He admitted that he really was not a soldier, and that he had no desire to be one, but the generals he had had in the past seemed incapable of action on their own, and so totally unconscious of the political pressures upon the government, that he had been forced essentially to be his own general-in-chief. Grant listened politely, assured the president that he would indeed act, and went away, keeping his own counsel.

Ulysses S. Grant now commanded some 550,000 men in a whole welter of commands. It was impossible both to administer this number and to direct it operationally, so he retained Henry Halleck as his chief of staff, at last finding the position for which Old Brains was actually suited. Grant's war strategy called for two main offensives, and a number of supplementary operations. First of all, he recognized that the character of the war had changed; it was a fight to the finish, and it could be won only by destroying the Confederate will to fight. That in turn could be accomplished either by depriving the Confederacy of the resources with which to sustain the struggle, which was desirable, or by killing Confederates, which was lamentable but necessary. To this end he told Meade: Your object is Robert Lee's army; you go where he goes; fight him and destroy him. He told Sherman the same thing: Destroy Johnston's army.

James L. Stokesbury, *A Short History of the Civil War.* New York: W. Morrow, 1995.

ported by telegraph to the department commander the information I had received, and added that I was taking steps to get off that night to be in advance of the enemy in securing that important point. There was a large number of steamers lying at Cairo and a good many boatmen were staying in the town. It was the work of only a few hours to get the boats manned, with coal aboard and steam up. Troops were also designated to go aboard. The distance from Cairo to Paducah is about forty-five miles. I did not wish to get there before daylight of the 6th [of September 1861], and directed therefore that the boats should lie at anchor out in the stream until the time to start. Not having received an answer to my first dispatch, I again telegraphed to department headquarters that I should start for Paducah that night unless I received further orders. Hearing nothing, we started before midnight and arrived early the following morning, anticipating the enemy by probably not over six or eight hours. . . .

When the National troops entered the town the citizens were taken by surprise. I never after saw such consternation depicted on the faces of the people. Men, women and children came out of their doors looking pale and frightened at the presence of the invader. They were expecting rebel troops that day. In fact, nearly four thousand men from Columbus were at that time within ten or fifteen miles of Paducah on their way to occupy the place. I had but two regiments and one battery with me; but the enemy did not know this and returned to Columbus. I stationed my troops at the best points to guard the roads leading into the city, left gunboats to guard the river fronts and by noon was ready to start on my return to Cairo. Before leaving, however, I addressed a short printed proclamation to the citizens of Paducah assuring them of our peaceful intentions, that we had come among them to protect them against the enemies of our country, and that all who chose could continue their usual avocations with assurance of the protection of the government. This was evidently a relief to them; but the majority would have much preferred the presence of the other army.

One Officer's Opinion

Robert Gould Shaw

More than a year had passed since the firing on Fort Sumter, and still the Union armies had scored no victories over their Confederate opponents. Washington politicians and Northern citizens were not the only ones grumbling about the national army—many officers, in private, expressed the belief that the troops were being led by incompetents.

In a letter home to his mother, Colonel Robert Gould Shaw, the commander of the war's most famous black regiment, the 54th Massachusetts, expresses his disgust with Congress and the President, whose interference in army training and discipline is prolonging the end of the war, at a great cost to time, life, and money.

Washington, Va.
July 23, 1862
Dear Mother,

As I mentioned in a short note to Father day before yesterday, I have received several letters from home since we arrived here. Yesterday I got his of 18th July. I was very sorry to hear you had not been well. I hope you are careful about exposing yourself.

Now Congress has adjourned, perhaps the war will be more vigorously and systematically carried on, though I think we should do better still, if the President and his Cabinet would adjourn too. Our republican government never

Excerpted from Robert Gould Shaw's letter to his mother dated July 23, 1862.

managed the country with a very firm hand, even in time of peace, and one year of war has shown pretty clearly that that is not its forte. We may finish the war, but it will certainly be with a much greater loss of time, life, and money than if we had had some men, any man almost, with a few common-sense military ideas, to manage matters, without being meddled with and badgered by a lot of men who show the greatest ignorance about the commonest things. Who but a crazy man could have stopped the enlisting, because there were 700,000 men mustered into the service? Taking out of these the sick, the deserters, and those on detached service in hospitals, barracks, &c., we couldn't have more than 500,000 before the campaign began. All these were scattered about the country, and we had no reserve, or recruiting stations to draw from. . . .

A Need for Discipline

I see that the papers are all crying out and wondering because there are at least forty thousand men absent and unaccounted for, who should be with McClellan, or this army. What is the reason they can go off with impunity and be out of the way, just when they are wanted? Because when it was

A group of Union officers are shown at their headquarters. The dearth of Union victories had some officers calling for better organization and discipline among the troops.

necessary to shoot some men last winter for desertion, the President pardoned them, and every one thought it was too bad to punish our "brave Volunteers" for just going home to see their families for a little while, without permission. They know now that nothing will be done to them, and many of them are deserting to enlist in the new regiments for $100 bounty [cash payment made for enlisting, set by the U.S. Congress in July, 1861]. The same policy has been followed with the army all along.

Senator Wilson [Henry Wilson of Massachusetts] makes a great fuss because some of his constituents are court-martialed and condemned to the Washington Penitentiary, for what he calls "trifling offences." One "trifling offence" is leaving the ranks on the march. The regiment goes into a fight after four hours marching, and only two thirds or one half of the men are present. This may seem a "trifling offence" to some men, but it certainly is not. Men mustn't be severely punished for disobeying orders, for deserting, for insulting and even striking their officers and non-commissioned officers, and the result is that they do just about what they please. If the majority of them hadn't more intelligence and good sense than most members of Congress, the army would be in a very bad condition, or rather, much worse than it is now. I think this is partly due to the custom of allowing men to elect their own officers, who consequently have little control over them, and partly to the interference of government with our commanders in the management of their troops. . . .

If we were sure of having a perfectly disinterested and patriotic man, what a good thing it would be to appoint a dictator in time of war. I begin to think I had rather have one at any rate, than see things go on as they do now.

Why the North Must Fight

William T. Sherman

In September of 1864, Union army major-general William T. Sherman prepared to destroy the crucial Confederate railway junction and manufacturing center of Atlanta, Georgia. Before burning Atlanta, Sherman issued an order for the city to be completely evacuated. The order brought an appeal from city officials, who asked Sherman to reconsider for the sake of civilian women, children, and the elderly. In the following letter to Mayor James M. Calhoun and city council members E.E. Rawson and S.C. Wells, Sherman refuses to delay the evacuation and explains why Atlanta must be destroyed. Sherman's harsh philosophy of war-making is later summed up in history books by his most famous saying, "War is hell!"

Headquarters Military Division of the Mississippi in the Field, Atlanta, Georgia, James M. Calhoun, Mayor, E.E. Rawson and S.C. Wells, representing City Council of Atlanta.

Gentleman: I have your letter of the 11th, in the nature of a petition to revoke my orders removing all the inhabitants from Atlanta. I have read it carefully, and give full credit to your statements of distress that will be occasioned, and yet shall not revoke my orders, because they were not designed to meet the humanities of the case, but to prepare for the future struggles in which millions of good people outside of Atlanta have a deep interest. We must have *peace*, not only

William T. Sherman, letter to the mayor and city council of Atlanta, Georgia, September 22, 1864 (Washington, DC: Union Congressional Committee, 1864).

at Atlanta, but in all America. To secure this, we must stop
the war that now desolates our once happy and favored
country. To stop war, we must defeat the rebel armies which
are arrayed against the laws and Constitution that all must
respect and obey. To defeat those armies, we must prepare
the way to reach them in their recesses, provided with the
arms and instruments which enable us to accomplish our
purpose. Now, I know the vindictive nature of our enemy,
that we may have many years of military operations from
this quarter; and, therefore, deem it wise and prudent to prepare in time. The use of Atlanta for warlike purposes is in-
consistent with its character as a home for families. There
will be no manufacturers, commerce, or agriculture here, for
the maintenance of families, and sooner or later want will
compel the inhabitants to go. Why not *go now*, when all the
arrangements are completed for the transfer, instead of waiting till the plunging shot of contending armies will renew
the scenes of the past month? Of course, I do not apprehend
any such thing at this moment, but you do not suppose this
army will be here until the war is over. I cannot discuss this
subject with you fairly, because I cannot impart to you what
we propose to do, but I assert that our military plans make
it necessary for the inhabitants to go away, and I can only
renew my offer of services to make their exodus in any direction as easy and comfortable as possible.

"War Is Cruelty"

You cannot qualify war in harsher terms than I will. War is
cruelty, and you cannot refine it; and those who brought war
into our country deserve all the curses and maledictions a
people can pour out. I know I had no hand in making this
war, and I know I will make more sacrifices to-day than any
of you to secure peace. But you cannot have peace and a division of our country. If the United States submits to a division now, it will not stop, but will go on until we reap the fate
of Mexico, which is eternal war. The United States does and
must assert its authority, wherever it once had power; for, if
it relaxes one bit to pressure, it is gone, and I believe that

Major-General William T. Sherman (seated, center), shown with other Union generals, prepares to lead the destruction of Atlanta, Georgia, a manufacturing and rail center of great importance to the South.

such is the national feeling. This feeling assumes various shapes, but always comes back to that of Union. Once admit the Union, once more acknowledge the authority of the national Government, and, instead of devoting your houses and streets and roads to the dread uses of war, I and this army become at once your protectors and supporters, shielding you from danger, let it come from what quarter it may. I know that a few individuals cannot resist a torrent of error and passion, such as swept the South into rebellion, but you can point out, so that we may know those who desire a government, and those who insist on war and its desolation.

You might as well appeal against the thunder-storm as against these terrible hardships of war. They are inevitable, and the only way the people of Atlanta can hope once more to live in peace and quiet at home, is to stop the war, which can only be done by admitting that it began in error and is perpetuated in pride.

We don't want your Negroes, or your horses, or your lands, or any thing you have, but we do want and will have a just obedience to the laws of the United States. That we will have, and if it involves the destruction of your improvements, we cannot help it.

"When Peace Does Come, You May Call on Me for Anything"

You have heretofore read public sentiment in your newspapers, that live by falsehood and excitement; and the quicker you seek for truth in other quarters, the better. I repeat then that, by the original compact of government, the United States had certain rights in Georgia, which have never been relinquished and never will be; that the South began the war by seizing forts, arsenals, mints, custom-houses, etc., etc., long before Mr. Lincoln was installed, and before the South had one jot or tittle of provocation. I myself have seen in Missouri, Kentucky, Tennessee, and Mississippi, hundreds and thousands of women and children fleeing from your armies and desperadoes, hungry and with bleeding feet. In Memphis, Vicksburg, and Mississippi, we fed thousands upon thousands of the families of rebel soldiers left on our hands, and whom we could not see starve. Now that war comes to you, you feel very different. You deprecate its horrors, but did not feel them when you sent carloads of soldiers and ammunition, and moulded shells and shot, to carry war into Kentucky and Tennessee, to desolate the homes of hundreds and thousands of good people who only asked to live in peace at their old homes, and under the Government of their inheritance. But these comparisons are idle. I want peace, and believe it can only be reached through union and war, and I will ever conduct war with a view to perfect an early success.

But, my dear sirs, when peace does come, you may call on me for anything. Then will I share with you the last cracker, and watch with you to shield your homes and families against danger from every quarter.

Now you must go, and take with you the old and feeble, feed and nurse them, and build for them, in more quiet places, proper habitations to shield them against the weather until the mad passions of men cool down, and allow the Union and peace once more to settle over your old homes in Atlanta. Yours in haste,

W.T. Sherman, *Major-General commanding*

Life in Andersonville Prison

John Ransom

Captured by the Confederates in the summer of 1863, quartermaster John Ransom of the 23rd Michigan was shipped to Andersonville, Georgia, site of the Confederacy's most notorious and deadly prisoner-of-war camp. Originally designed to hold 10,000 prisoners, Andersonville's prison population swelled to more than 32,000 by August 1864. It is estimated that nearly 13,000 Union soldiers died there.

John Ransom's Andersonville diary became one of the best-known eyewitness accounts of Civil War prison life. In a simple and direct manner, Ransom tells of hunger, disease, crime, savagery, and death; while hundreds around him are suffering and dying like animals, he manages to keep his sympathy with and understanding of human nature.

July 3.—Three hundred and fifty new men from West Virginia were turned into this summer resort this morning. They brought good news as to successful termination of the war, and they also caused war after coming among us. As usual the raiders [camp gangsters] proceeded to rob them of their valuables and a fight occurred in which hundreds were engaged. The cut throats came out ahead. Complaints were made to Capt. Wirtz [Andersonville commander] that this thing would be tolerated no longer, that these raiders must be put down or the men would rise in their might and break away if assistance was not given with which to preserve or-

Excerpted from *Andersonville Diary*, by John Ransom (Cincinnati: Douglass Bros. & Payne, 1883).

der. Wirtz flew around as if he had never thought of it before, issued an order to the effect that no more food would be given us until the leaders were arrested and taken outside for trial. The greatest possible excitement. Hundreds that have before been neutral and non-commital are now joining a police force. Captains are appointed to take charge of the squads which have been furnished with clubs by Wirtz. As I write, this middle of the afternoon, the battle rages. The police go right to raider headquarters knock right and left and make their arrests. Sometimes the police are whipped and have to retreat, but they rally their forces and again make a charge in which they are successful. Can lay in our shade and see the trouble go on. Must be killing some by the shouting. The raiders fight for their very life, and are only taken after being thoroughly whipped. The stockade is loaded with guards who are fearful of a break. I wish I could describe the scene to-day. A number killed. After each arrest a great cheering takes place. *Night.*—Thirty or forty of the worst characters in camp have been taken outside, and still the good work goes on. No food to-day and don't want any. A big strapping fellow called Limber Jim heads the police. Grand old Michael Hoare is at the front and goes for a raider as quick as he would a rebel. Patrol the camp all the time and gradually quieting down. The orderly prisoners are feeling jolly.

July 4.—The men taken outside yesterday are under rebel guard and will be punished. The men are thoroughly aroused, and now that the matter has been taken in hand, it will be followed up to the letter. Other arrests are being made to-day, and occasionally a big fight. Little Terry, whom they could not find yesterday, was to-day taken. Had been hiding in an old well, or hole in the ground. Fought like a little tiger, but had to go. "Limber Jim" is a brick, and should be made a Major General if he ever reaches our lines. Mike Hoare is right up in rank, and true blue. Wm. B. Rowe also makes a good policeman, as does "Dad" Sanders. Battese says he "no time to fight, must wash." Jimmy Devers regrets that he cannot take a hand in, as he likes to fight, and especially with a club. The writer hereof does no fighting, being on the sick list. The excitement of looking on is most too much for me. Can hardly arrest the big graybacks [lice] crawling around. Capt. Moseby is one of the arrested ones. His right name is Collins and he has been in our hundred all the time since leaving Richmond. Has got a good long neck to stretch. Another man whom I have seen a good deal of, one Curtiss, is also arrested. I haven't mentioned poor little Bullock for months, seems to me. He was most dead when we first came to Andersonville, and is still alive and tottering around. Has lost his voice entirely and is nothing but a skeleton. Hardly enough of him for disease to get hold of. Would be one of the surprising things on record if he lives through it, and he seems no worse than months ago. It is said that a court will be formed of our own men to try the raiders. Any way, so they are punished. All have killed men, and they themselves should be killed. When arrested, the police had hard work to prevent their being lynched. Police more thoroughly organizing all the time. An extra amount of food this P.M., and police get extra rations, and three out of our mess is doing pretty well, as they are all willing to divide. They tell us all the encounters they have, and much interesting talk. Mike has some queer experiences. Rebel flags at half mast for some of their great men. Just heard that the trial of raiders will begin to-morrow.

July 5.—Court is in session outside and raiders being tried by our own men. Wirtz has done one good thing, but it's a question whether he is entitled to any credit, as he had to be threatened with a break before he would assist us. Rations again to-day. I am quite bad off with my diseases, but still there are so many thousands so much worse off that I do not complain much, or try not to however.

July 6.—Boiling hot, camp reeking with filth, and no sanitary privileges; men dying off over a hundred and forty per day. Stockade enlarged, taking in eight or ten more acres, giving us more room, and stumps to dig up for wood to cook with. Mike Hoare is in good health; not so Jimmy Devers. Jimmy has now been a prisoner over a year, and poor boy, will probably die soon. Have more mementoes than I can carry, from those who have died, to be given to their friends at home. At least a dozen have given me letters, pictures &c., to take North. Hope I shan't have to turn them over to some one else.

July 7.—The court was gotten up by our own men and from our own men; Judge, jury, counsel. &c. Had a fair trial, and were even defended, but to no purpose. It is reported that six have been sentenced to be hung, while a good many others are condemned to lighter punishment, such as setting in the stocks, strung up by the thumbs, thumb screws, head hanging, etc. The court has been severe, but just. Mike goes out to-morrow to take some part in the court proceedings. The prison seems a different place altogether; still, dread disease is here, and mowing down good and true men. Would seem to me that three or four hundred died each day, though officially but one hundred and forty odd is told. About twenty-seven thousand, I believe, are here now in all. No new ones for a few days. Rebel visitors, who look at us from a distance. It is said the stench keeps all away who have no business here and can keep away. Washing business good. Am negotiating for a pair of pants. Dislike fearfully to wear dead men's clothes, and haven't to any great extent.

July 8.—Oh, how hot, and oh, how miserable. The news that six have been sentenced to be hanged is true, and one of them is Moseby. The camp is thoroughly under control of the police now, and it is a heavenly boon. Of course there is some stealing and robbery, but not as before. Swan, of our mess, is sick with scurvy. I am gradually swelling up and growing weaker. But a few more pages in my diary. Over a hundred and fifty dying per day now, and twenty six thousand in camp. Guards shoot now very often. Boys, as guards, are the most cruel. It is said that if they kill a Yankee, they are given a thirty days furlough. Guess they need them as soldiers too much to allow of this. The swamp now is fearful, water perfectly reeking with prison offal and poison. Still men drink it and die. Rumors that the six will be hung inside. Bread to-day and it is so coarse as to do more hurt than good to a majority of the prisoners. The place still gets worse. Tunneling is over with; no one engages in it now that I know of. The prison is a success as regards safety; no escape except by death, and very many take advantage of that way. A man who has preached to us (or tried to) is dead. Was a good man I verily believe, and from Pennsylvania. It's almost impossible for me to get correct names to note down; the last named man was called "the preacher," and I can find no other name for him. Our quartette of singers a few rods away is disbanded. One died, one nearly dead, one a policeman and the other cannot sing alone, and so where we used to hear and enjoy good music evenings, there is nothing to attract us from the groans of the dying. Having formed a habit of going to sleep as soon as the air got cooled off and before fairly dark, I wake up at two or three o'clock and stay awake. I then take in all the horrors of the situation. Thousands are groaning, moaning and crying, with no bustle of the daytime to drown it. Guards every half hour call out the time and post, and there is often a shot to make one shiver as if with the ague. Must arrange my sleeping hours to miss getting owly in the morning. Have taken to building air castles of late, on being exchanged [freed in exchange for confederate prisoners in Union camps]. Getting loony, I guess, same as all the rest.

July 11.—This morning lumber was brought into the prison by the rebels, and near the gate a *gallows* erected for the purpose of executing the six condemned Yankees. At about ten o'clock they were brought inside by [Confederate] Capt. Wirtz and some guards, and delivered over to the police force. Capt. Wirtz then said a few words about their having been tried by our own men and for us to do as we choose with them, that he washed his hands of the whole matter, or words to that effect. I could not catch the exact language, being some little distance away. I have learned by enquiry, their names, which are as follows: John Sarsfield, 144th New York; William Collins, alias "Moseby," Co. D, 88th Pennsylvania; Charles Curtiss, Battery A, 5th Rhode Island Artillery; Pat Delaney, Co. E, 83d Pennsylvania; A. Munn, U.S.

Navy, and W.R. Rickson of the U. S. Navy. After Wirtz made his speech he withdrew his guards, leaving the condemned at the mercy of 28,000 enraged prisoners who had all been more or less wronged by these men. Their hands were tied behind them, and one by one they mounted the scaffold. Curtiss, who was last, a big stout fellow, managed to get his hands loose and broke away and ran through the crowd and down toward the swamp. It was yelled out that he had a knife in his hand, and so a path was made for him. He reached the swamp and plunged in, trying to get over on the other side, presumably among his friends. It being very warm he over exerted himself, and when in the middle or thereabouts, collapsed and could go no farther. The police started after him, waded in and helped him out. He pleaded for water and it was given him. Then led back to the scaffold and helped to mount up. All were given a chance to talk. Munn, a good looking fellow in marine dress, said he came into the prison four months before perfectly honest, and as innocent of crime as any fellow in it. Starvation, with evil companions, had made him what he was. He spoke of his mother and sisters in New York, that he cared nothing as far as he himself was concerned, but the news that would be carried home to his people made him want to curse God he had ever been born. Delaney said he would rather be hung than live here as the most of them lived, on their allowance of rations. If allowed to steal could get enough to eat, but as that was stopped had rather hang. Bid all good bye. Said his name was not Delaney and that no one knew who he really was, therefore his friends would never know his fate, his Andersonville history dying with him. Curtiss said he didn't care a—only hurry up and not be talking about it all day; making too much fuss over a very small matter. William Collins alias Moseby, said he was innocent of murder and ought not to be hung; he had stolen blankets and rations to preserve his own life, and begged the crowd not to see him hung as he had a wife and child at home, and for their sake to let him live. The excited crowd began to be impatient for the "show" to commence as they termed it. Sarsfield made quite a speech; he had studied for a lawyer; at the outbreak of the rebellion he had enlisted and served three years in the army, been wounded in battle, furloughed home, wound healed up, promoted to first sergeant and also commissioned; his commission as a lieutenant had arrived but had not been mustered in when he was taken prisoner; began by stealing parts of rations, gradually becoming hardened as he became familiar with the crimes practiced; evil associates had helped him to go down hill and here he was. The other did not care to say anything. While the men were talking they were interrupted by all kinds of questions and charges made by the crowd, such as "don't lay it on too thick, you villain," "get ready to jump off," "cut it short," "you was the cause of so and so's death," "less talk and more hanging," &c., &c. At about eleven o'clock they were all blindfolded, hands and feet tied, told to get ready, nooses adjusted and the plank knocked from under. Moseby's rope broke and he fell to the ground, with blood spurting from his ears, mouth and nose. As they was lifting him back to the swinging off place he revived and begged for his life, but no use, was soon dangling with the rest, and died very hard. Munn died easily, as also did Delaney, all the rest died hard and particularly Sarsfield who drew his knees nearly to his chin and then straightened them out with a jerk, the veins in his neck swelling out as if they would burst. It was an awful sight to see, still a necessity. Moseby, although he said he had never killed any one, and I don't believe he ever did deliberately kill a man, such as stabbing or pounding a victim to death, yet he has walked up to a poor sick prisoner on a cold night and robbed him of blanket, or perhaps his rations and if necessary using all the force necessary to do it. These things were the same as life to the sick man, for he would invariably die. The result has been that many have died from his robbing propensities. It was right that he should hang, and he did hang most beautifully and Andersonville is the better off for it. None of the rest denied that they had killed men, and probably some had murdered dozens. It has been a good lesson; there are still bad ones in camp but we have the strong arm of the law to keep them in check. All during the hanging scene the stockade was covered with rebels, who were fearful a break would be made if the raiders should try and rescue them. Many citizens too were congregated on the outside in favorable positions for seeing. Artillery was pointed at us from all directions, ready to blow us all into eternity in short order; Wirtz stood on a high platform in plain sight of the execution and says we are a hard crowd to kill our own men. After hanging for half an hour or so the six bodies were taken down and carried outside. In noting down the speeches made by the condemned men, have used my own language; in substance it is the same as told by them. I occupied a near position to the hanging and saw it all from first to last, and stood there until they were taken down and carried away. Was a strange sight to see and the first hanging I ever witnessed. The raiders had many friends who crowded around and denounced the whole affair and but for the police there would have been a riot; many both for and against the execution were knocked down. Some will talk and get into trouble thereby; as long as it does no good there is no use in loud talk and exciting arguments; is dangerous to advance any argument, men are so ready to quarrel. Have got back to my quarters thoroughly prostrated and worn out with fatigue and excitement, and only hope that to-day's lesson will right matters as regards raiding. Battese suspended washing long enough to look on and see them hang and grunted his approval. Have omitted to say that the good Catholic priest attended the condemned. Rebel negroes came inside and began to take down the scaffold; prisoners took hold to help them and resulted in its all being carried off to different parts of the prison to be used for kindling wood, and the rebels get none of it back and are mad. The ropes even have been gobbled up, and I suppose sometime may be exhibited at the north as mementoes of to-day's proceedings. Mike Hoare assisted at the hanging. Some fears are entertained that those who officiated will get killed by the friends of those hanged. The person who manipulated the "drop," has been taken outside on parole [word] of honor [not to fight for the Union], as his life would be in danger in here. Jimmy thanks God that he has lived to see justice done the raiders; he is about gone—nothing but skin and bone and can hardly move hand or foot; rest of the mess moderately well. The extra rations derived from our three mess-mates as policemen, helps wonderfully to prolong life. Once in a while some of them gets a chance to go outside on some duty and buy onions or sweet potatoes which is a great luxury.

July 12.—Good order has prevailed since the hanging. The men have settled right down to the business of dying, with no interruption. I keep thinking our situation can get no worse, but it does get worse every day and not less than one hundred and sixty die each twenty-four hours. Probably one-fourth or one-third of these die inside the stockade, the balance in the hospital outside. All day and up to four o'-clock P.M., the dead are being gathered up and carried to the south gate and placed in a row inside the dead line. As the bodies are stripped of their clothing in most cases as soon as the breath leaves, and in some cases before, the row of dead presents a sickening appearance. Legs drawn up and in all shapes. They are black from pitch pine smoke and lay-ing in the sun. Some of them lay there for twenty hours or more, and by that time are in a horrible condition. At four o'clock a four or six mule wagon comes up to the gate and twenty or thirty bodies are loaded on to the wagon and they are carted off to be put in trenches, one hundred in each trench, in the cemetery, which is eighty or a hundred rods away. There must necessarily be a great many whose names are not taken. It is the orders to attach the name, company and regiment to each body, but it is not always done. I was invited to-day to dig in a tunnel, but had to decline. My dig-ging days are over. Must dig now to keep out of the ground, I guess. It is with difficulty now that I can walk, and only with the help of two canes.

July 13.—Can see in the distance the cars [trains] go pok-ing along by this station, with wheezing old engines, snorting along. As soon as night comes a great many are blind, caused by sleeping in the open air, with moon shining in the face.

Many holes are dug and excavations made in camp. Near our quarters is a well about five or six feet deep, and the poor blind fellows fall into this pit hole. None seriously hurt, but must be quite shaken up. Half of the prisoners have no settled place for sleeping, wander and lay down wherever they can find room. Have two small gold rings on my finger, worn ever since I left home. Have also a small photograph album with eight photographs in. Relics of civilization. Should I get these things through to our lines they will have quite a history. When I am among the rebels I wind a rag around my finger to cover up the rings, or else take them and put in my pocket. Bad off as I have been, have never seen the time yet that I would part with them. Were presents to me, and the photographs have looked at about one-fourth of the time since imprisonment. One prisoner made some buttons here for his little boy at home, and gave them to me to deliver, as he was about to die. Have them sewed on to my pants for safe keeping.

Showing What One Is

July 14.—We have been too busy with the raiders of late to manufacture any exchange news, and now all hands are at work trying to see who can tell the biggest yarns. The weak are feeling well to-night over the story that we are all to be sent North this month, before the 20th. Have not learned that the news came from any reliable source. Rumors of midsummer battles with Union troops victorious. It's "bite dog, bite bear," with most of us prisoners; we don't care which licks, what we want is to get out of this pen. Of course, we all care and want our side to win, but it's tough on patriotism. A court is now held every day and offenders punished, principally by buck and gagging, for misdemeanors. The hanging has done worlds of good, still there is much stealing going on yet, but in a sly way, not openly. Hold my own as regards health. The dreaded month of July is half gone, almost, and a good many over one hundred and fifty die each day, but I do not know how many. Hardly any one cares enough about it to help me any in my inquiries. It is all self with the most of them. A guard by accident shot himself. Have often said they didn't know enough to hold a gun. Bury a rebel guard every few days within sight of the prison. Saw some women in the distance. Quite a sight. Are feeling quite jolly to-night since the sun went down. Was visited by my new acquaintances of the 9th Michigan Infantry, who are comparatively new prisoners. Am learning them the way to live here. They are very hopeful fellows and declare the war will be over this coming fall, and tell their reasons very well for thinking so. We gird up our loins and decide that we will try to live it through. Rowe, although often given to despondency, is feeling good and cheerful. There are some noble fellows here. A man shows exactly what he is in Andersonville. No occasion to be any different from what you really are. Very often see a great big fellow in size, in reality a baby in action, actually sniveling and crying, and then again you will see some little runt, "not bigger than a pint of cider," tell the big fellow to "brace up" and be a man. Stature has nothing to do as regards nerve, still there are noble big fellows as well as noble little ones. A Sergt. Hill is judge and jury now, and dispenses justice to evil doers with impartiality. A farce is made of defending some of the arrested ones. Hill inquires all of the particulars of each case, and sometimes lets the offenders go as more sinned against than sinning. Four receiving punishment.

July 15.—Blank cartridges were this morning fired over the camp by the artillery, and immediately the greatest commotion outside. It seems that the signal in case a break is made, is cannon firing. And this was to show us how quick they could rally and get into shape. In less time than it takes for me to write it, all were at their posts and in condition to open up and kill nine-tenths of all here. Sweltering hot. Dying off one hundred and fifty-five each day. There are twenty-eight thousand confined here now.

July 16.—Well, who ever supposed that it could be any hotter; but to-day is more so than yesterday, and yesterday more than the day before. My coverlid has been rained on so much and burned in the sun, first one and then the other, that it is getting the worse for wear. It was originally a very nice one, and home made. Sun goes right through it now, and reaches down for us. Just like a bake oven. The rabbit mules that draw in the rations look as if they didn't get much more to eat than we do. Driven with one rope line, and harness patched up with ropes, strings, &c. Fit representation of the Confederacy. Not much like U.S. Army teams. A joke on the rebel adjutant has happened. Some one broke into the shanty and tied the two or three sleeping there, and carried off all the goods. Tennessee Bill, (a fellow captured with me) had charge of the affair, and is in disgrace with the adjutant on account of it. Every one is glad of the robbery. Probably there was not ten dollars worth of things in there, but they asked outrageous prices for everything. Adjt. very mad, but no good. Is a small, sputtering sort of fellow.

July 17.—Cords [cramps] contracting in my legs and very difficult for me to walk—after going a little ways have to stop and rest and am faint. Am urged by some to go to the hospital but don't like to do it; mess say had better stay where I am, and Battese says shall not go, and that settles it. Jimmy Devers anxious to be taken to the hospital but is persuaded to give it up. Tom McGill, another Irish friend, is past all recovery; is in another part of the prison. Many old prisoners are dropping off now this fearful hot weather; knew that July and August would thin us out; cannot keep track of them in my disabled condition. A fellow named Hubbard with whom I have conversed a good deal, is dead; a few days ago was in very good health, and it's only a question of a few days now with any of us. Succeeded in getting four small onions about as large as hickory nuts, tops and all for two dollars Confederate money. Battese furnished the money but won't eat an onion; ask him if he is afraid it will make his breath smell? It is said that two or three onions or a sweet potato eaten raw daily will cure the scurvy. What a shame that such things are denied us, being so plenty the world over. Never appreciated such things before but shall hereafter. Am talking as if I expected to get home again. I do.

July 18.—Time slowly dragging itself along. Cut some wretches's hair most every day. Have a sign out "Hair Cutting," as well as "Washing," and by the way, Battese has a new wash board made from a piece of the scaffold lumber. About half the time do the work for nothing, in fact not more than one in three or four pays anything—expenses not much though, don't have to pay any rent. All the mess keeps their hair cut short which is a very good advertisement. My eyes getting weak with other troubles. Can just hobble around. Death rate more than ever, reported one hundred and sixty-five per day; said by some to be more than that, but 165 is about the figure. Bad enough without making any worse than it really is. Jimmy Devers most dead and begs us to take him to the hospital and guess will have to. Every morning the sick are carried to the gate in blankets and on stretchers, and the worst cases admitted to the hospital. Probably out of five or six hundred half are admitted. Do not think any lives after being taken there; are past all human aid. Four out of every five prefer to stay inside and die with their friends rather than go to the hospital. Hard stories reach us of the treatment of the sick out there and I am sorry to say the cruelty emanates from our own men who act as nurses. These dead beats and bummer nurses are the same bounty jumpers the U.S. authorities have had so much trouble with [those who enlist solely for payment of a bounty, then desert]. Do not mean to say that all the nurses are of that class but a great many of them are.

July 19.—There is no such thing as delicacy here. Nine out of ten would as soon eat with a corpse for a table as any other way. In the middle of last night I was awakened by being kicked by a dying man. He was soon dead. In his struggles he had floundered clear into our bed. Got up and moved the body off a few feet, and again went to sleep to dream of the hideous sights. I can never get used to it as some do. Often wake most scared to death, and shuddering from head to foot. Almost dread to go to sleep on this account. I am getting worse and worse, and prison ditto.

Losing Friends

July 20.—Am troubled with poor sight together with scurvy and dropsy. My teeth are all loose and it is with difficulty I can eat. Jimmy Devers was taken out to die to-day. I hear that McGill is also dead. John McGuire died last night, both were Jackson men and old acquaintances. Mike Hoare is still policeman and is sorry for me. Does what he can. And so we have seen the last of Jimmy. A prisoner of war one year and eighteen days. Struggled hard to live through it, if ever any one did. Ever since I can remember have known him. John Maguire also, I have always known. Everybody in Jackson, Mich., will remember him, as living on the east side of the river near the wintergreen patch, and his father before him. They were one of the first families who settled that country. His people are well-to-do, with much property. Leaves a wife and one boy. Tom McGill is also a Jackson boy and a member of my own company. Thus you will see that three of my acquaintances died the same day, for Jimmy cannot live until night I don't think. Not a person in the world but would have thought either one of them would kill me a dozen times enduring hardships. Pretty hard to tell about such things. Small squad of poor deluded Yanks turned inside with us, captured at Petersburg. It is said they talk of winning recent battles. Battese has traded for an old watch and Mike will try to procure vegetables for it from the guard. That is what will save us if anything.

July 21.—And rebels are still fortifying. Battese has his hands full. Takes care of me like a father. Hear that Kilpatrick is making a raid for this place. Troops (rebel) are arriving here by every train to defend it. Nothing but corn bread issued now and I cannot eat it any more.

July 22.—A petition is gotten up signed by all the sergeants in the prison, to be sent to Washington, D.C., *begging* to be released. Capt. Wirtz has consented to let three representatives go for that purpose. Rough that it should be necessary for us to *beg* to be protected by our government.

July 23.—Reports of an exchange in August. Can't stand it till that time. Will soon go up the spout.

July 24.—Have been trying to get into the hospital, but Battese won't let me go. Geo. W. Hutchins, brother of Charlie Hutchins of Jackson, Mich., died to-day—from our mess.

Jimmy Devers is dead.

July 25.—Rowe getting very bad. Sanders ditto. Am myself much worse, and cannot walk, and with difficulty stand up. Legs drawn up like a triangle, mouth in terrible shape, and dropsy worse than all. A few more days. At my earnest solicitation was carried to the gate this morning, to be admitted to the hospital. Lay in the sun for some hours to be examined, and finally my turn came and I tried to stand up, but was so excited I fainted away. When I came to myself I lay along with the row of dead on the outside. Raised up and asked a rebel for a drink of water, and he said: "Here, you Yank, if you ain't dead, get inside there!" And with his help was put inside again. Told a man to go to our mess and tell them to come to the gate, and pretty soon Battese and Sanders came and carried me back to our quarters; and here I am, completely played out. Battese flying around to buy me something good to eat. Can't write much more. Exchange rumors.

July 26.—Ain't dead yet. Actually laugh when I think of the rebel who thought if I wasn't dead I had better get inside. Can't walk a step now. Shall try for the hospital no more. Had an onion.

July 27.—Sweltering hot. No worse than yesterday. Said that two hundred die now each day. Rowe very bad and Sanders getting so. Swan dead, Gordon dead, Jack Withers dead, Scotty dead, a large Irishman who has been near us a long time is dead. These and scores of others died yesterday and day before. Hub Dakin came to see me and brought an onion. He is just able to crawl around himself.

July 28.—Taken a step forward toward the trenches since yesterday, and am worse. Had a wash all over this morning. Battese took me to the creek; carries me without any trouble.

July 29.—Alive and kicking. Drank some soured water made from meal and water.

July 30.—Hang on well, and no worse.

Chapter 4

The Black Soldier in the Northern Army

Chapter Preface

The firing on Fort Sumter inspired thousands of free African Americans to volunteer their services for the Union cause. But even as the Southern states seceded from the Union and mustered armies to the fronts, a federal statute dating to 1792 prohibited blacks from service in the United States military.

The Lincoln administration feared dire consequences if blacks were allowed to fight for the Union. It was thought that blacks would make poor and undisciplined soldiers, and that integration would anger whites in the military. In addition, the administration believed that recruiting blacks would turn Northern civilians against the war and prompt the still-undecided border states to join the Confederacy.

As the war continued, however, and it grew apparent that the Union army would win no easy victory, more manpower was needed. On September 22, 1862, President Lincoln issued a preliminary Emancipation Proclamation, and recruitment of black soldiers into the Union army began. By May 1863, the government had established the Bureau of Colored Troops to organize the thousands of black men volunteering for service.

During the Civil War, about 180,000 African-American men served in the Union army, and 20,000 in the United States Navy. Black regiments suffered 40,000 deaths, most of them due to the diseases that raged through crowded and unhealthy encampments. They also suffered from poor training and leadership, which translated into confusion and indecisiveness on the battlefield. The issue most nettlesome to black troops, however, was unequal pay. Not until July 1864, did Congress finally grant black troops pay and clothing allowances equal to those of white soldiers.

Despite the discrimination they often suffered, black regiments performed heroically during the Civil War. In the best-known battle in which black troops took part, the siege of Fort Wagner, South Carolina, the 54th Massachusetts Volunteers lost half of its men and two-thirds of its officers. In other, less famous engagements, however, African-American enlisted men proved themselves the equal in courage and ability to their white counterparts in the Union army.

Life in a Black Regiment

Thomas Wentworth Higginson

> Before the outbreak of the Civil War, Thomas Higginson of Massachusetts, a Unitarian minister, had dedicated himself to the cause of abolition. When the war began, he took command of the nation's first African-American regiment, the 1st South Carolina. The unit first saw action along the St. John's River in northern Florida. After retiring from service in 1864, Colonel Higginson set down his experiences in *Army Life in a Black Regiment*, including these entries from his wartime diaries.

C amp Saxton, near Beaufort, S.C., November 24, 1862.

Yesterday afternoon we were steaming over a summer sea, the deck level as a parlor-floor, no land in sight, no sail, until at last appeared one light-house, said to be Cape Romaine, and then a line of trees and two distant vessels and nothing more. The sunset, a great illuminated bubble, submerged in one vast bank of rosy suffusion; it grew dark; after tea all were on deck, the people sang hymns; then the moon set, a moon two days old, a curved pencil of light, reclining backwards on a radiant couch which seemed to rise from the waves to receive it; it sank slowly, and the last tip wavered and went down like the mast of a vessel of the skies. Towards morning the boat stopped, and when I came on deck, before six,—

Excerpted from *Army Life in a Black Regiment*, by Thomas Wentworth Higginson (Boston: Fields, Osgood, 1870).

"The watch-lights glittered on the land,
The ship-lights on the sea."

Hilton Head lay on one side, the gunboats on the other; all that was raw and bare in the low buildings of the new settlement was softened into picturesqueness by the early light. Stars were still overhead, gulls wheeled and shrieked, and the broad river rippled duskily towards Beaufort.

The shores were low and wooded, like any New England shore; there were a few gunboats, twenty schooners, and some steamers, among them the famous "Planter," which Robert Small, the slave, presented to the nation. The riverbanks were soft and graceful, though low, and as we steamed up to Beaufort on the flood-tide this morning, it seemed almost as fair as the smooth and lovely canals which Stedman traversed to meet his negro soldiers in Surinam. The air was cool as at home, yet the foliage seemed green, glimpses of stiff tropical vegetation appeared along the banks, with great clumps of shrubs, whose pale seed-vessels looked like tardy blossoms. Then we saw on a picturesque point an old plantation, with stately magnolia avenue, decaying house, and tiny church amid the woods, reminding me of Virginia; behind it stood a neat encampment of white tents, "and there," said my companion, "is your future regiment."

Three miles farther brought us to the pretty town of Beaufort, with its stately houses amid Southern foliage. Reporting to General Saxton, I had the luck to encounter a company of my destined command, marched in to be mustered into the United States service. They were unarmed, and all looked as thoroughly black as the most faithful philanthropist could desire; there did not seem to be so much as a mulatto among them. Their coloring suited me, all but the legs, which were clad in a lively scarlet, as intolerable to my eyes as if I had been a turkey. I saw them mustered; General Saxton talked to them a little, in his direct, manly way; they gave close attention, though their faces looked impenetrable. Then I conversed with some of them. The first to whom I spoke had been wounded in a small expedition after lumber, from which a party had just returned, and in

which they had been under fire and had done very well. I
said, pointing to his lame arm,—

"Did you think that was more than you bargained for, my
man?"

His answer came promptly and stoutly,—

"I been a-tinking, Mas'r, *dat's jess what I went for.*"

I thought this did well enough for my very first interchange of dialogue with my recruits.

November 27, 1862.

Thanksgiving-Day; it is the first moment I have had for
writing during these three days, which have installed me
into a new mode of life so thoroughly that they seem three
years. Scarcely pausing in New York or in Beaufort, there
seems to have been for me but one step from the camp of a
Massachusetts regiment to this, and that step over leagues
of waves.

It is a holiday wherever General Saxton's proclamation
reaches. The chilly sunshine and the pale blue river seem
like New England, but those alone. The air is full of noisy
drumming, and of gunshots; for the prize-shooting is our
great celebration of the day, and the drumming is chronic.
My young barbarians are all at play. I look out from the broken windows of this forlorn plantation-house, through av-
enues of great live-oaks, with their hard, shining leaves, and
their branches hung with a universal drapery of soft, long
moss, like fringe-trees struck with grayness. Below, the
sandy soil, scantly covered with coarse grass, bristles with
sharp palmettoes and aloes; all the vegetation is stiff, shining, semi-tropical, with nothing soft or delicate in its tex-
ture. Numerous plantation-buildings totter around, all
slovenly and unattractive, while the interspaces are filled
with all manner of wreck and refuse, pigs, fowls, dogs, and
omnipresent Ethiopian infancy. All this is the universal
Southern panorama; but five minutes' walk beyond the hov-
els and the live-oaks will bring one to something so un-
Southern that the whole Southern coast at this moment trem-
bles at the suggestion of such a thing,—the camp of a
regiment of freed slaves.

One adapts one's self so readily to new surroundings that already the full zest of the novelty seems passing away from my perceptions, and I write these lines in an eager effort to retain all I can. Already I am growing used to the experience, at first so novel, of living among five hundred men, and scarce a white face to be seen,—of seeing them go through all their daily processes, eating, frolicking, talking, just as if they were white. Each day at dress-parade I stand with the customary folding of the arms before a regimental line of countenances so black that I can hardly tell whether the men stand steadily or not; black is every hand which moves in ready cadence as I vociferate, "Battalion! Shoulder arms!" nor is it till the line of white officers moves forward, as parade is dismissed, that I am reminded that my own face is not the color of coal.

The first few days on duty with a new regiment must be devoted almost wholly to tightening reins; in this process one deals chiefly with the officers, and I have as yet had but little personal intercourse with the men. They concern me chiefly in bulk, as so many consumers of rations, wearers of uniforms, bearers of muskets. But as the machine comes into shape, I am beginning to decipher the individual parts. At first, of course, they all looked just alike; the variety comes afterwards, and they are just as distinguishable, the officers say, as so many whites. Most of them are wholly raw, but there are many who have already been for months in camp in the abortive "Hunter Regiment," yet in that loose kind of way which, like average militia training, is a doubtful advantage. I notice that some companies, too, look darker than others, though all are purer African than I expected. This is said to be partly a geographical difference between the South Carolina and Florida men. When the Rebels evacuated this region they probably took with them the house-servants, including most of the mixed blood, so that the residuum [rest] seems very black. But the men brought from Fernandina the other day average lighter in complexion, and look more intelligent, and they certainly take wonderfully to the drill.

It needs but a few days to show the absurdity of distrusting the military availability of these people. They have quite as much average comprehension as whites of the need of the thing, as much courage (I doubt not), as much previous knowledge of the gun, and, above all, a readiness of ear and of imitation, which, for purposes of drill, counterbalances any defect of mental training. To learn the drill, one does not want a set of college professors; one wants a squad of eager, active, pliant school-boys; and the more childlike these pupils are the better. There is no trouble about the drill; they will surpass whites in that. As to camp-life, they have little to sacrifice; they are better fed, housed, and clothed than ever in their lives before, and they appear to have few inconvenient vices. They are simple, docile, and affectionate almost to the point of absurdity. The same men who stood fire in open field with perfect coolness, on the late expedition, have come to me blubbering in the most irresistibly ludicrous manner on being transferred from one company in the regiment to another.

In noticing the squad-drills I perceive that the men learn less laboriously than whites that "double, double, toil and trouble," which is the elementary vexation of the drill-master,—that they more rarely mistake their left for their right,—and are more grave and sedate while under instruction. The extremes of jollity and sobriety, being greater with them, are less liable to be intermingled; these companies can be driven with a looser rein than my former one, for they restrain themselves; but the moment they are dismissed from drill every tongue is relaxed and every ivory tooth visible. This morning I wandered about where the different companies were target-shooting, and their glee was contagious. Such exulting shouts of "Ki! ole man," when some steady old turkey-shooter brought his gun down for an instant's aim, and then unerringly hit the mark; and then, when some unwary youth fired his piece into the ground at half-cock, such infinite guffawing and delight, such rolling over and over on the grass, such dances of ecstasy, as made the "Ethiopian minstrelsy" of the stage appear a feeble imitation. . . .

December 1, 1862.

How absurd is the impression bequeathed by Slavery in regard to these Southern blacks, that they are sluggish and inefficient in labor! Last night, after a hard day's work (our guns and the remainder of our tents being just issued), an order came from Beaufort that we should be ready in the evening to unload a steamboat's cargo of boards, being some of those captured by them a few weeks since, and now assigned for their use. I wondered if the men would grumble at the night-work; but the steamboat arrived by seven, and it was bright moonlight when they went at it. Never have I beheld such a jolly scene of labor. Tugging these wet and heavy boards over a bridge of boats ashore, then across the slimy beach at low tide, then up a steep bank, and all in one great uproar of merriment for two hours. Running most of the time, chattering all the time, snatching the boards from each other's backs as if they were some coveted treasure, getting up eager rivalries between different companies, pouring great choruses of ridicule on the heads of all shirkers, they made the whole scene so enlivening that I gladly stayed out in the moonlight for the whole time to watch it. And all this without any urging or any promised reward, but simply as the most natural way of doing the thing. The steamboat captain declared that they unloaded the ten thousand feet of boards quicker than any white gang could have done it; and they felt it so little, that, when, later in the night, I reproached one whom I found sitting by a campfire, cooking a surreptitious opossum, telling him that he ought to be asleep after such a job of work, he answered, with the broadest grin,—

"O no, Cunnel, da's no work at all, Cunnel; dat only jess enough *for stretch we*."

December 2, 1862.

I believe I have not yet enumerated the probable drawbacks to the success of this regiment, if any. We are exposed to no direct annoyance from the white regiments, being out of their way; and we have as yet no discomforts or privations which we do not share with them. I do not as yet see the slightest obstacle, in the nature of the blacks, to making them good soldiers, but rather the contrary. They take readily to drill, and do not object to discipline; they are not especially dull or inattentive; they seem fully to understand the importance of the contest, and of their share in it. They show no jealousy or suspicion towards their officers.

They do show these feelings, however, towards the Government itself; and no one can wonder. Here lies the drawback to rapid recruiting. Were this a wholly new regiment, it would have been full to overflowing, I am satisfied, ere now. The trouble is in the legacy of bitter distrust bequeathed by the abortive regiment of General Hunter,—into which they were driven like cattle, kept for several months in camp, and then turned off without a shilling, by order of the War Department. The formation of that regiment was, on the whole, a great injury to this one; and the men who came from it, though the best soldiers we have in other respects, are the least sanguine and cheerful; while those who now refuse to enlist have a great influence in deterring others. Our soldiers are constantly twitted by their families and friends with their prospect of risking their lives in the service, and being paid nothing; and it is in vain that we read them the instructions of the Secretary of War to General Saxton, promising them the full pay of soldiers. They only half believe it.

Another drawback is that some of the white soldiers delight in frightening the women on the plantations with doleful tales of plans for putting us in the front rank in all battles, and such silly talk,—the object being, perhaps, to prevent our being employed on active service at all. All these considerations they feel precisely as white men would,—no less, no more; and it is the comparative freedom from such unfavorable influences which makes the Florida men seem more bold and manly, as they undoubtedly do. To-day General Saxton has returned from Fernandina with seventy-six recruits, and the eagerness of the captains to secure them was a sight to see. Yet they cannot deny that some of the very best men in the regiment are South Carolinians.

December 3, 1862.—7 P.M.

What a life is this I lead! It is a dark, mild, drizzling evening, and as the foggy air breeds sand-flies, so it calls out melodies and strange antics from this mysterious race of grown-up children with whom my lot is cast. All over the camp the lights glimmer in the tents, and as I sit at my desk in the open doorway, there come mingled sounds of stir and glee. Boys laugh and shout,—a feeble flute stirs somewhere in some tent, not an officer's,—a drum throbs far away in another,—wild kildeer-plover flit and wail above us, like the haunting souls of dead slave-masters,—and from a neighboring cook-fire comes the monotonous sound of that strange festival, half pow-wow, half prayer-meeting, which they know only as a "shout." These fires are usually enclosed in a little booth, made neatly of palm-leaves and covered in at top, a regular native African hut, in short, such as is pictured in books, and such as I once got up from dried palm-leaves for a fair at home. This hut is now crammed with men, singing at the top of their voices, in one of their quaint, monotonous, endless, negro-Methodist chants, with obscure syllables recurring constantly, and slight variations interwoven, all accompanied with a regular drumming of the feet and clapping of the hands, like castanets. Then the excitement spreads: inside and outside the enclosure men begin to quiver and dance, others join, a circle forms, winding monotonously round some one in the centre; some "heel and toe" tumultuously, others merely tremble and stagger on, others stoop and rise, others whirl, others caper sideways, all keep steadily circling like dervishes; spectators applaud special strokes of skill; my approach only enlivens the scene; the circle enlarges, louder grows the singing, rousing shouts of encouragement come in, half bacchanalian, half devout, "Wake 'em, brudder!" "Stan' up to 'em, brudder!"— and still the ceaseless drumming and clapping, in perfect cadence, goes steadily on. Suddenly there comes a sort of *snap,* and the spell breaks, amid general sighing and laughter. And this not rarely and occasionally, but night after night, while in other parts of the camp the soberest prayers and exhortations are proceeding sedately.

A simple and lovable people, whose graces seem to come by nature, and whose vices by training. Some of the best superintendents confirm the first tales of innocence, and Dr. Zachos told me last night that on his plantation, a sequestered one, "they had absolutely no vices." Nor have these men of mine yet shown any worth mentioning; since I took command I have heard of no man intoxicated, and there has been but one small quarrel. I suppose that scarcely a white regiment in the army shows so little swearing. Take the "Progressive Friends" [Abolitionists] and put them in red trousers, and I verily believe they would fill a guard-house sooner than these men. If camp regulations are violated, it seems to be usually through heedlessness. They love passionately three things besides their spiritual incantations; namely, sugar, home, and tobacco. This last affection brings tears to their eyes, almost, when they speak of their urgent need of pay; they speak of their last-remembered quid [tobacco plug] as if it were some deceased relative, too early lost, and to be mourned forever. As for sugar, no white man can drink coffee after they have sweetened it to their liking.

I see that the pride which military life creates may cause the plantation trickeries to diminish. For instance, these men make the most admirable sentinels. It is far harder to pass the camp lines at night than in the camp from which I came; and I have seen none of that disposition to connive at the offences of members of one's own company which is so troublesome among white soldiers. Nor are they lazy, either about work or drill; in all respects they seem better material for soldiers than I had dared to hope.

There is one company in particular, all Florida men, which I certainly think the finest-looking company I ever saw, white or black; they range admirably in size, have remarkable erectness and ease of carriage, and really march splendidly. Not a visitor but notices them; yet they have been under drill only a fortnight, and a part only two days. They have all been slaves, and very few are even mulattoes.

A Plea for Equal Pay

James Gooding

In the spring of 1863, two years into the Civil War, the United States government finally granted African Americans the right to fight for the Union. Yet that decision did not bring about equal treatment or pay for black soldiers. They received $7 a month plus a $3 per month clothing allowance, while white soldiers earned $13 per month plus a $3.50 per month clothing allowance. One black regiment, the 54th Massachusetts, refused any pay whatsoever to protest this discrimination.

On September 28, 1863, Corporal James Gooding wrote the following letter to President Lincoln, setting down the arguments for equality of pay as well as opportunity. In July 1864, the Congress granted this request, and in September of that year the men of the 54th Massachusetts received all back pay due them.

Your Excellency, Abraham Lincoln:
Your Excellency will pardon the presumption of a humble individual like myself in addressing you, but the earnest solicitation of my comrades in arms, besides the genuine interest felt by myself in the matter, is my excuse for placing before the executive head of the nation our common grievance.

On the 6th of the last month [August, 1863], the paymaster of the department informed us that if we would decide to receive the sum of $10 (ten dollars) per month, he would come and pay us that sum, but that, on the sitting of Congress, the regiment would, in his opinion, be allowed

James H. Gooding, letter to Abraham Lincoln, September 28, 1863 (Washington, DC: National Archives).

the other $3 (three). He did not give us any guarantee that this would be as he hoped; certainly *he* had no authority for making any such guarantee, and we cannot suppose him acting in any way interested.

Now the main question is, are we *soldiers* or are we *laborers?* We are fully armed and equipped; have done all the various duties pertaining to a soldier's life; have conducted ourselves to the complete satisfaction of general officers who were, if any, prejudiced *against* us, but who now accord us all the encouragement and honor due us; have shared the perils and labor of reducing the first stronghold that flaunted a traitor flag; and more, Mr. President, today the Anglo-Saxon mother, wife, or sister are not alone in tears for departed sons, husbands, and brothers. The patient, trusting descendants of Africa's clime have dyed the ground with blood in defense of the Union and democracy. Men, too, Your Excellency, who know in a measure the cruelties of the iron heel of oppression, which, in years gone by, the very power their blood is now being spilled to maintain, ever ground them to the dust.

But when the war trumpet sounded o'er the land, when men knew not the friend from the traitor, the black man laid his life at the altar of the nation—and he was refused. When the arms of the Union were beaten, in the first year of the war, and the executive called for more food for its ravaging maw, again the black man begged the privilege of aiding his country in her need—to be again refused.

A Soldier's Duty

And now he is in the war, and how has he conducted himself? Let their dusky forms rise up out the mires of James Island and give the answer. Let the rich mold around [Fort] Wagner's parapets be upturned, and there will be found an eloquent answer. Obedient and patient and solid as a wall are they. All we lack is a paler hue and a better acquaintance with the alphabet.

Now, Your Excellency, we have done a soldier's duty. Why can't we have a soldier's pay? You caution the Rebel chieftain that the United States knows no distinction in her soldiers. She insists on having all her soldiers of whatever creed or color to be treated according to the usages of war. Now, if the United States exacts uniformity of treatment of her soldiers from the insurgents, would it not be well and consistent to set the example herself by paying all her *soldiers* alike?

We of this regiment were not enlisted under any "contraband" act. But we do not wish to be understood as rating our service of more value to the government than the service of the ex-slave. Their service *is* undoubtedly worth much to the nation, but Congress made express provision touching their case, as slaves freed by military necessity, and assuming the government to be their temporary guardian. Not so with us. Freemen by birth and consequently having the advantage of *thinking* and acting for ourselves so far as the laws would allow us, we do not consider ourselves fit subjects for the contraband act.

We appeal to you, sir, as the executive of the nation, to have us justly dealt with. The regiment do pray that they be assured their service will be fairly appreciated by paying them as American *soldiers,* not as menial hirelings. Black men, you may well know, are poor; $3 per month, for a year, will supply their needy wives and little ones with fuel. If you, as chief magistrate of the nation, will assure us of our whole pay, we are content. Our patriotism, our enthusiasm will have a new impetus to exert our energy more and more to aid our country. Not that our hearts ever flagged in devotion, spite the evident apathy displayed in our behalf, but we feel as though our country spurned us, now we are sworn to serve her. Please give this a moment's attention.

Racist and Incompetent Leaders

Benjamin Williams

It was not unusual for African Americans to encounter racism in military as well as civilian life. The 32nd U.S. Colored Infantry, stationed at Morris Island, South Carolina, provides one example, as many of its members wrote home describing the general incompetence, maltreatment, and poor leadership exhibited by its officers.

In a letter home, Benjamin Williams gives a vivid account of the harsh conditions at this isolated post, many of which he attributes to the refusal of the volunteers to take the meager pay then being offered to black troops. Williams takes some consolation in the courage and steadfastness shown by his brother soldiers, all determined to resolutely face the Confederates despite the trouble in their own encampment.

We arrived at Sea Brook, eight miles up the creek, west of Hilton Head [South Carolina]. There we were ordered to encamp. We stayed there one week. We had nothing to eat but oysters and five hard tacks [bread rations] a day, that we picked up along the shore. As usual, after we had fixed up our camp so nicely; order came for us to strike tents and march, which was promptly executed. We marched back to Hilton Head and took the steamer Cosmopolitan, and reported at Folly Island, and marched to Morris Island, where we are still in camp near Fort Shaw. We are encamped on the old hospital ground, where they buried all

Excerpted from Benjamin Williams, letter to the editor, *Christian Recorder*, July 30, 1864.

their dead. We had to dig wells in the graveyard, and drink the water off the putrid bodies, and it is killing our men.

The health of the men in general, is as well as can be expected. We have lost ten men since our departure, and among the brave hearts was that of Jesse Dexter, the Quartermaster Sergeant, who leaves a wife and child to mourn his loss.

The paymaster has made us a visit, and offered us seven dollars a month, which all of the men refused, except a few in the left wing, who sneaked up at night and signed the pay roll; but the majority of the men would sooner stay their time out and do without the seven dollars. Our officers seem very much put out, and beg the men to take it. They said that the next day we would get all that is coming to us, and said, "Boys, we think that you had better take the money." But we told them that it was a big thing on ice, but we could not see it; and, after the officers found out that the men would not take the seven dollars, they began to treat those men like dogs. The least thing that the men would do, they were bucked and gagged, and put on knapsack drill, and made to stand in the hot, broiling sun for four hours at a stretch; in consequence of which, a few of the men got sunstruck.

Our Brave Officers

We have drills and dress-parades and battalion drills, which none of our officers know anything about. When they are ordered by a command, they don't know how to do it. One night we went out on picket duty. Every thing went on well all through the night, and in the morning, when the pickets were taken off, the rebels began to shell and cross-fire. Our brave officers sent the men on ahead and they stayed behind, because they were afraid of the rebels' shells, and, when they came down to camp they were under arrest for their cowardice. The officer in command told them that they had not as much heart as their men had, and that the regiment would be better drilled if they had the officers to command them, but they had not an officer in the regiment that knew his business and knew how to do his duty, and that the regiment was hardly worth the rations that they drew. And there is our drum-corps, that we brought with us from Philadelphia. They have not got their uniforms yet, and they are the worst corps on the island. They are laughed at and sneered at by all the other regiments. We know it is not the fault of the drum-major. It is the fault of the commanding officers. The General says that if we were to go into the field with such officers as we now have, we would all get cut to pieces, and that there is no use taking us into action until our officers have learned a little more.

Mr. Editor, it looks hard that a party of men should treat colored men in this way. There is our gentlemanly doctor. He is a very nice man, indeed. He has not got any medicine fit to give the men. If they get very sick in their quarters, the doctor will order them brought to the hospital where they will not be more than twenty-four hours before they are dead. That is the way the men are served. Dr. [Charles] Wight growls and snaps at the men as if they were dogs, and he says, if the men are not fit for duty; send them to him and he will soon get them out of the way; for he says it is no harm to kill a nigger.

When the regiment first encamped here, we were treated more like soldiers; but as soon as we refused to take seven dollars a month, they commenced to treat us like dogs. Before the Paymaster came around, there was not anything like bucking and gagging; but as soon as we refused to take the pay, they commenced. They even bucked and gagged a boy because he happened not to have the seat of his pants sewed up for inspection. It was impossible for him to sew them up, as he had no money to buy a needle and thread with.

Not Fit for a Dog to Eat

Now, Mr. Editor, don't you think this is bad treatment for a Pennsylvania regiment to get? I think it is ridiculous and a shame before God and man. There was not a group that left Camp William Penn with such a set of officers as the Thirty-second United States Colored Troops. Look at the Forty-third Regiment United States Colored Troops, which was raised after we were. They have been brigaded and are now acting as rear-guard over the baggage train of the Army of the Potomac, whilst we are not fit for anything but to do all of the picket duty and drudgery work on the island; and we don't get our rations as we ought to. All the rations that are condemned by the white troops are sent to our regiment. You ought to see the hard tack that we have to eat. They are moldy and musty and full of worms, and not fit for a dog to eat, and the rice and beans and peas are musty and the salt horse (the salt beef, I mean) is so salty that, after it is cooked, we can't eat it. Some days the men are sent on fatigue in the hot sun, and when they come home to dinner, there is nothing to eat but rotten hard tack and flat coffee, without sugar in it.

Now, Mr. Editor, if this is not killing men, I don't know what is. There is one thing that I had almost forgotten. It is concerning the Sergeant-Major of the regiment. He made his boasts and went around bragging to the men in camp that he would not take seven dollars a month; and before he would take it he would stay out his three years and do without it, and he hoped that no man in the regiment would take it. But when the paymaster came, he changed his tune, and signed his name to the pay roll, and took the seven dollars. The next day he looked like a man that had done some great deed. Only look at it, he holding the highest non-commissioned office that a colored man can hold. We would not think so hard of it if he had been a private. He is one of your Philadelphia sports, and bears the title of Sergeant-Major George W. Clemens.

An Appraisal of Black Troops

Nathaniel Banks

Whites of both North and South doubted the fighting ability, discipline, and courage of black soldiers. Many of these doubts were put to rest during the siege of Port Hudson, Louisiana, when General Nathaniel Banks led a stubborn attack on a fortified Confederate position in May 1863.

Here is General Banks' appraisal of his troops, as expressed in a letter to General Henry Halleck. The letter was first published as part of *Washington and Jackson on Negro Soldiers*, a pamphlet advocating black enlistment into the Union army and printed in Philadelphia in 1863.

HEADQUARTERS ARMY OF THE GULF,
BEFORE PORT HUDSON, MAY 30, 1863.

Major-General H. W. Halleck, General-in-Chief,
Washington.

GENERAL:—Leaving Sommesport [Louisiana] on the Atchafalaya, where my command was at the date of my last dispatch, I landed at Bayou Sara at 2 o'clock on the morning of the 21st.

A portion of the infantry were transported in steamers, and the balance of the infantry, artillery, cavalry, and wagon train moving down on the west bank of the river, and from this to Bayou Sara.

On the 23d a junction was effected with the advance of Major-General AUGUR and Brigadier-General SHERMAN, our

Nathaniel Banks, letter to H.W. Halleck, May 30, 1863.

line occupying the Bayou Sara road at a distance five miles from Port Hudson.

Major-General AUGUR had an encounter with a portion of the enemy on the Bayou Sara road in the direction of Baton Rouge, which resulted in the repulse of the enemy, with heavy loss.

On the 25th the enemy was compelled to abandon his first line of works.

Assault Along Sandy Creek

General WEITZEL'S brigade, which had covered our rear in the march from Alexandria, joined us on the 26th, and on the morning of the 27th a general assault was made upon the fortifications.

The artillery opened fire between 5 and 6 o'clock, which was continued with animation during the day. At 10 o'clock WEITZEL'S brigade, with the division of General GROVER, reduced to about two brigades, and the division of General EMORY, temporarily reduced by detachments to about a brigade, under command of Colonel PAINE, with two regiments of colored troops, made an assault upon the right of the enemy's works, crossing Sandy Creek, and driving them through the woods to their fortifications.

The fight lasted on this line until 4 o'clock, and was very severely contested. On the left, the infantry did not come up until later in the day; but at 2 o'clock an assault was opened on the centre and left of centre by the divisions under Major-General AUGUR and Brigadier-General SHERMAN.

The enemy was driven into his works, and our troops moved up to the fortifications, holding the opposite sides of the parapet with the enemy on the right. Our troops still hold their position on the left. After dark the main body, being exposed to a flank fire, withdrew to a belt of woods, the skirmishers remaining close upon the fortifications.

In the assault of the 27th, the behavior of the officers and men was most gallant, and left nothing to be desired. Our limited acquaintance of the ground and the character of the works, which were almost hidden from our obser-

The Attack on Fort Wagner

At first, soldiers and civilians of the North looked askance on the idea of putting African American volunteers in uniform. But a series of fierce battles, in which black troops gave a good account of themselves, changed the public's opinion. The most famous of these was the assault on Battery Wagner, a Confederate fortification in Charleston harbor. Herman Hattaway, author of Shades of Blue and Gray, *describes the near-suicidal attack carried out by the famous 54th Massachusetts on July 18, 1863.*

In their desperate and unsuccessful attempt to capture the battery, which was never *taken* (the Confederates elected to abandon it on September 6, 1863), the Fifty-fourth Massachusetts paid a fearful price. The task of taking Battery Wagner was nearly an impossible one; the place was a huge and powerful earth fort built across the narrow neck of Morris Island at the harbor's mouth. No flanking approach was possible. Ground troops had no avenue of assault but a frontal one. Unobstructed fields of fire were buttressed by massive implantations of land mines. The Confederate inventor Gen. Gabriel Rains had been sent to Battery Wagner to give special attention to the defenses and to the deployment of torpedoes equipped with his new and quite potent Rains fuse. Sand offered perfect camouflage, completely obscuring the shallow emplacement of deadly devices detonated as if by a hair trigger. Though some of the attackers got the regimental colors up to the parapets, they could not penetrate nor could they stay, and the survivors were forced to retreat. The Fifty-fourth Massachusetts lost more than 40 percent of its number, including its prominent young colonel [Col. Robert Gould Shaw], who was buried in a mass grave with the black soldiers who fell with him.

Herman Hattaway, *Shades of Blue and Gray.* Columbia, MO: University of Missouri Press, 1997.

vation until the moment of approach, alone prevented the capture of the post.

The Utmost Bravery

On the extreme right of our line I posted the first and third regiments of negro troops. The First regiment of Louisiana Engineers, composed exclusively of colored men, excepting the officers, was also engaged in the operations of the day. The position occupied by these troops was one of importance, and called for the utmost steadiness and bravery in those to whom it was confided.

It gives me pleasure to report that they answered every expectation. Their conduct was heroic. No troops could be more determined or more daring. They made, during the day, three charges upon the batteries of the enemy, suffering very heavy losses, and holding their position at nightfall with the other troops on the right of our line. The highest commendation is bestowed upon them by all the officers in command on the right. Whatever doubt may have existed before as to the efficiency of organizations of this character, the history of this day proves conclusively to those who were in a condition to observe the conduct of these regiments, that the Government will find in this class of troops effective supporters and defenders.

The severe test to which they were subjected, and the determined manner in which they encountered the enemy, leave upon my mind no doubt of their ultimate success. They require only good officers, commands of limited numbers, and careful discipline, to make them excellent soldiers.

Our losses from the 23d to this date in killed, wounded, and missing, are nearly 1000, including, I deeply regret to say, some of the ablest officers of the corps. I am unable yet to report them in detail.

I have the honor to be, with much respect,
> Your obedient servant,
> > N.P. BANKS, *Major-General Commanding.*

Chapter 5

On the Home Front

Chapter Preface

The Civil War was a total war, one that involved civilians as well as soldiers on both sides. Families throughout the North could no longer farm or carry on business in the usual way, as their every action and decision was measured by its effect on the war effort. Northerners, thanks to efficient communications, were able to follow events closely. Newspapers carried dispatches that arrived directly from the fronts via telegraph. Illustrators depicted the battles and other incidents of the war in magazines, and photographs taken by Matthew Brady and others created a graphic and authentic record of the death and destruction wrought by armed conflict.

In this war, there were no neutral parties. Every civilian took a stand, either for or against the war, and as the conflict dragged on through 1864 and 1865, the disruption and bitter feelings between opposing sides grew worse. The conflict divided thousands of families, especially in the border states of Maryland, Kentucky, and Missouri. Brothers and cousins found themselves bearing arms for opposite sides. Even a town or region solidly for one side or the other found itself at risk from members of secret organizations, who riding at night, burned the homes and fields of their opponents. The war also brought old ethnic hatreds to the surface. Rioting whites in New York and other cities killed hundreds of free African Americans, and hatred among Irish, Germans, Chinese, and other immigrant groups also sparked deadly violence.

Not everyone in the North supported the war. Some, such as the Society of Friends (or Quakers) objected to the war altogether on religious grounds. The Quakers stood against violence in any form and declared themselves not subject to the military draft on the grounds of being "conscientious objectors." Political opponents were also outspoken in their opinions. Others objected to Lincoln's conduct of the war. One faction in Congress, known as the Radical Republicans, thought Lincoln moved too slowly and cautiously on the issue of freeing the slaves. On the other side were the Copperheads, those who argued against Lincoln's stand for the Union. Some Copperheads called for a negotiated peace, while others believed the North should adopt the Confederate constitution.

In this atmosphere of conflicting ideas and goals, a temporary suspension of the liberties guaranteed by the Constitution and the Bill of Rights seemed necessary. President Lincoln gave federal officers the authority to imprison draft-evaders and Southern sympathizers at will, while the courts suspended the right of habeas corpus (the legal right to a hearing and trial upon being imprisoned and charged). In some instances, the suspension of due process also led to the removal of Union opponents from holding office even after a free and fair election. The most famous Copperhead leader, Clement L. Vallandinghan of Ohio, was arrested, tried by a military court, and banished from the North for the duration of the war for his political views.

Quantrill's Raiders Attack Lawrence

Gurdon Grovenor

During the Civil War, Confederate guerrilla bands roamed far and wide on the western frontier, disrupting Northern supply routes, burning depots, robbing mail trains and coaches, capturing runaway slaves, and attacking civilians. The most notorious of these raiders was William C. Quantrill, a former schoolteacher whose extracurricular activities included horse stealing, theft and murder. In 1862, the Confederate army commissioned him a captain and made his band into a regular unit of the Confederate army.

Targeted for special attention by Confederate raiders were towns and settlements known for their sympathies toward the Union cause. In August, 1863, Quantrill and 450 of his followers swooped down on Lawrence, Kansas, a city established and settled by committed Northern abolitionists. The result was a day and night of fighting, destruction, and utter terror for the civilian inhabitants of Lawrence, as described in the following account by the eyewitness Gurdon Grovenor.

It was a clear, warm, still morning, in the midst of one of the hot, dry, dusty spells of weather common in Kansas in the month of August. The guerrillas reached Lawrence just before sunrise after an all night's ride from the border of Missouri. Myself and family were yet in bed and asleep. They passed directly by our house, and we were awakened by their yelling and shouting.

Reprinted from a memoir of Gurdon Grovenor, August 1863.

Terror in the Streets

I thought at first that the noise came from a company of colored recruits who were camped just west of our house; thought that they had got to quarrelling among themselves. I got up and went to the window to see what was the matter, and as I drew aside the curtain the sight that met my eyes was one of terror—one that I never shall forget. The bushwhackers were just passing by my house. There were 350 of them, all mounted and heavily armed; they were grim and dirty from their night's ride over the dusty roads and were a reckless and bloodthirsty set of men. It was a sight we had somewhat anticipated, felt that it might come, and one that we had dreaded ever since the commencement of the war. I turned to my wife and said: "The bushwhackers are here."

They first made for the main street, passing up as far as the Eldridge House to see if they were going to meet with any opposition, and when they found none they scattered out all over town, killing, stealing and burning. We hastily dressed ourselves and closed up the house tightly as possible and began to talk over what was best to do. My first thought was to get away to some hiding place, but on looking out there seemed no possibility of that as the enemy were everywhere, and I had a feeling that I ought not to leave my family, a young wife and two children, one a babe of three months old, and so we sat down and awaited developments. We saw men shot down and fires shooting up in all directions.

Just on the north of our house, a half a block away and in full view was a camp of recruits twenty-two in all, not yet mustered into service and unarmed. They were awakened by the noise, got up and started to run but were all shot down but five. I saw this wholesale shooting from my window, and it was a sight to strike terror to a stouter heart than mine. But we had not long to wait before our time came. Three of the guerrillas came to the house, stepped up on the front porch, and with the butt of a musket smashed in one of the front windows; my wife opened the door and let them in. They ransacked the house, talked and swore and threatened a good deal, but offered no violence. They set the house on fire above and below, took such things as they fancied, and left. After they had gone I put the fire out below, but above it had got too strong a hold, and I could not put it out.

The Moment of Truth

Not long after a single man rode up to the front gate; he was a villainous looking fellow, and was doubly villainous from too much whiskey. He saw me standing back in the hall of the house, and with a terrible oath he ordered me to come out. I stepped out on the piazza, he leveled his pistol at me and said; "Are you union or secesh [secessionist]?"

It was my time of trial; my wife with her little one in her arms, and our little boy clinging to her side, was standing just a little ways from me. My life seemingly hung on my answer, my position may be imagined but it cannot be described. The thought ran through me like an electric shock, that I could not say that I was a secessionist, and deny my loyalty to my country; that I would rather die than to live and face that disgrace; and so I answered that I was a union man. He snapped his pistol but it failed to fire. I stepped back into the house and he rode around to the north door and met me there, and snapped his pistol at me again, and this time it failed. Was there a providence in this?

Just then a party of a half dozen of the raiders came riding towards the house from the north, and seeing my enemy, hallooed to him, "Don't shoot that man." They rode up to the gate and told me to come there; I did so and my would-be murderer came up to me and placed the muzzle of his revolver in my ear. It was not a pleasant place to be in, but the leader of the new crowd told him not to shoot, but to let me alone until be could inquire about me, so he asked me if I had ever been down in Missouri stealing niggers or horses; I told him "No that I never had been in Missouri, except to cross the state going and coming from the east." This seemed to be satisfactory so he told my old enemy to let me alone and not to kill me. This seemed to make him very angry, and he cursed me terribly, but I ventured to put my hand up and push away his revolver. The leader of the party then told me if I did not expect to get killed, I must get out of sight, that they were all getting drunk, and would kill everybody they saw; I told him that that was what I had wanted to do all the morning, but I could not; "Well," he says, "you must hide or get killed." And they all rode away.

When a Lie Is Not a Sin

After they had gone I told my wife that I would go into the cellar, and stay until the fire reached me, and if any more of the raiders inquired for me to tell them that I had been taken a prisoner and carried off. Some years ago I read an article in the *Sunday School Times*, saying that a lie under any circumstances was a sin. I thought then that I should like to see that writer try my experiences at the time of the raid and see what he would think then; I did not feel my lie a sin then and never have since.

The cellar of my house was under the [building's wing] and the fire was in the front and in the upper story. There was an outside bulk-head door, where I knew I could get out after the fire had reached the floor above me. I had not been in the cellar long before my wife came and said they had just killed my neighbor across the street.

Soon after the notorious Bill Anderson, passing by the house, saw my wife standing in the yard, stopped and commenced talking with her; told her how many men he had killed that morning, and inquiring where her husband was; she told him that he had been taken prisoner and carried away—was it my wife's duty to tell him the truth, tell him where I was and let him come and shoot me as he would a dog, which he would have done? Awhile after my wife came and said she thought the raiders had all gone, and so I came out of my prison just as the fire was eating through the floor over my head, thankful that I had passed through that dreadful ordeal and was safe.

Such was my experience during those four or five terrible hours. Our home and its contents was in ashes, but so thankful were we that my life was spared that we thought but little of our pecuniary loss. After the raiders had left and the people could get out on the street, a most desolate and sickening sight met their view. The whole business part of the town, except two stores, was in ashes. The bodies of dead men, some of them partly burned away, were laying in all directions. A large number of dwellings were burned to the ground, and the moaning of the grief stricken people was heard from all sides. Gen. Lane, who was in the city at the time, told me that he had been over the battleground of Gettysburg a few days before, but the sight was not so sickening as the one which the burned and sacked city of Lawrence presented. The exact number killed was never known, but it was about 150, many of them the best citizens.

Fighting the Copperheads

George E. Stephens

The Emancipation Proclamation, which became law on January 1, 1863, was the impetus for further conflict between abolitionists and the Northern pro-slavery faction known as the Copperheads. The debate was made even more complex and divisive when it was joined by free African Americans now demanding to take their place in the ranks of the Union army. While blacks by the thousands sought to enlist in the 54th Massachusetts and other all-black regiments, their participation in the war was fiercely opposed by those who still sympathized with the South.

The debate grew especially bitter in Pennsylvania, the state that saw more battles and bloodshed during the war than any other in the North. The Copperheads were strong in Pennsylvania, and when the enlistment drive began among the state's blacks, this pro-slavery faction mounted a campaign to discourage black enlistment and to discredit the worth of blacks as soldiers in the minds of the general public. By setting blacks against whites, the Copperheads also hoped to divide the North and offer the South a desperately needed advantage.

These strategies are eloquently described by George E. Stephens, a future member of the 54th Massachusetts, in a letter to Robert Hamilton, editor of *The Weekly Anglo-African,* a leading Northern journal of African American affairs.

Reprinted from George E. Stephens, letter to the editor, *Weekly Anglo-African*, April 11, 1863.

Philadelphia, [Pennsylvania]
April 2, 1863

M r. Editor:
One of the most impudent assumptions of authority
and a long string of the basest misrepresentations have been
perpetuated by a number of white men under the leadership
of one Frishmuth, an illiterate German, on the people of the
State of Pennsylvania; men who possess no record on the
question of anti-slavery, and have not the shadow of a claim
to the confidence and support of the colored men of this
State, and are regarded by every intelligent colored man in
the city as irresponsible militarily, pecuniarily, politically,
and socially. Many of these men claim to have held quite re-
cently commissions in either the regular or volunteer service
of the United States, and rumor, which seems to be well
founded, says that at least three of these men were cashiered
or dismissed from the service.

It will be remembered that just as soon as Gov. [John] Andrew [of Massachusetts] had obtained authority from the War
Department at Washington to raise colored regiments, a si-
multaneous response of the colored men of every State in the
North was made to the call of the noble old Bay State. Every
one of us felt it to be a high and holy duty to organize the first
regiment of the North at once, so that the irresistible argument of a first-class regiment of Northern colored men *en
route* for the seat of war might overwhelm or, if possible,
scatter to the four winds the prejudice against enlisting colored men in the army, and at the same time giving cheer to
the hearts of good and loyal men everywhere. But no sooner
did that hateful political reptile, the copperhead [Southern
sympathizer], discover the generous response and patriotism
which this call elicited, than the insidious and guilty work of
counteracting or neutralizing these pure and earnest mani-
festations, commenced. Every influence has been applied to
dishearten us; mobbed, as at Detroit and elsewhere, and in
every town and village kicked, spit upon and insulted. The
wily enemy knows full well that if they can impress on the
minds of the masses the notion that the whites of the North

are as bitter enemies as those of the South, it would be impossible to get a regiment of Northern colored men; then they would deride Massachusetts and the colored men, as they do Gen. Jim Lane of Kansas, for failing to realize certain promises and expectations regarding the promptness of our people to enlist, and yell like madmen, "niggers won't fight!"

Copperhead Arguments

I am right glad that the black brigade is rolling up so bright a record. May they continue to drive before them the buzzard foe! You meet these copperheads at every step, and when violence is not resorted to, they come [with] the friendship and counsellor dodge. They ask, "Are you going to enlist in the army?" Of course, you answer "Yes!" They continue, "Any colored gentleman who will go down South to fight is a fool. Every one of them that the rebels catch will be hanged, or sent into the Indigo mines, or cut up into mincemeat, or quartered and pickled, or spitted, or—or—What good is it going to do the colored people to go fight and lose their lives? Better stay home and keep out of harm's way."

These are the arguments that the copperheads insinuate into the ears of the credulous, the ignorant, and the timid. They do not tell you that the measure of the slaveholder's iniquity is completed; that the accumulated wrongs of two centuries are a thousand-fold more horrible than two centuries of war and massacre. They do not tell you that it were "better to die free, than live slaves"—that your wronged and outraged sisters and brethren are calling on you to take up arms and place your interests and your lives in the balance against their oppressors—that "your dead fathers speak to you from their graves," or "Heaven, as with a voice of thunder, calls on you to arise from the dust," and smite with an avenging hand the obdurate, cruel, and relentless enemy and traitor, who has trampled in the dust the flag of his country and whose life and sacred honor are pledged to wage an interminable war against your race.

Oh no, to tell us these truths would be to nerve our arms and fire our hearts for the noble struggle for country and liberty. Men and brethren! for the sake of honor, manhood and courage—in the name of God, of country, and of race, spit upon the base sycophants who thus dare to insult you. But these are silent influences which are at work. The open, tangible, bolder ones are now at work in Pennsylvania. She presents a wide theater for operations. Her colored population is more numerous than that of any other Northern State; and if the copperheads can neutralize this State, half of the object has been accomplished and the system has been thoroughly organized. Ever since Frederick Douglass's address appeared in the daily journals, these men have been holding meetings and stuffing the Philadelphia papers with false accounts of their glowing success and influence over the colored people.

A few weeks ago they caused an article to appear in the *Evening Bulletin* which stated that sixty thousand dollars had been promised to them by colored men in this city. At a meeting of colored men held at Philadelphia Institute on last Wednesday, two weeks ago, and upon which meeting Frishmuth and his associates introduced themselves, Mr. Rob't Jones, the secretary of the meeting, read this article and demanded who the parties were that had subscribed this money. The whole gang were confounded. Not a name could be offered and not one colored man said that he reposed any confidence in those men. They forced themselves upon us, and spoke of the inadvisibility of colored men enlisting in the Massachusetts regiment; that there would be authority given to them the next day to organize a colored brigade in Pennsylvania; that President Lincoln and Gov. Curtin were only arranging the preliminaries.

Frishmuth said he loved the colored man and wanted to be "de Moses ob de cullerd population"—forgetting that Moses belonged to the race which he led out of the house of Egyptian bondage. There were many colored ladies present at the meeting, yet one of those unprincipled men used the most profane and disgusting language. They belong to that ignorant class of white men who, knowing nothing of the sentiments and intelligence of colored men, labor under the hallucination that they can lead where they will we should go, and that if a white man should say to us, "You are a good nigger," we will be immediately overwhelmed with gratitude for the gracious condescension.

They have printed circulars, scattered among the colored people in Philadelphia and adjoining counties, calling on them to join the 1st Colored Penn. Brigade. They hold "officers' meetings" and report their proceedings to the daily papers. They told a friend this morning that they had not yet received authority to enlist colored men. Of course not. By what authority do they thus call upon the men of color of Pennsylvania to take up arms and thus mislead them and deceive the public? By these misrepresentations all through the State, the efforts of our people, in a military point of view, have been neutralized. Even so far west as Pittsburgh, the copperhead bait has been successful. Even Geo. B. Vashon has been gulled into participating in a war meeting in Pittsburgh, in response to what they were led to believe by the

The Gettysburg Address

On November 19, 1863, about 15,000 people gathered at Cemetery Ridge, on the battlefield at Gettysburg, Pennsylvania, to hear speeches for the dedication of a new military cemetery. After a two-hour speech by Edward Everett, President Lincoln rose to the podium and spoke for about two minutes. In the speech, known today as the Gettysburg Address, Lincoln gave eloquent voice to the sacrifices of the fallen and to the determination to carry through the terrible war for the sake of a noble cause.

Four score and seven years ago our fathers brought forth on this continent a new nation, conceived in liberty and dedicated to the proposition that all men are created equal. Now we are engaged in a great civil war, testing whether that nation or any nation so conceived and so dedicated can long endure. We are met on a great battlefield of that war. We have

Philadelphia press, was a genuine call of Pennsylvania. We shall tear the curtain away, and expose to the people these gross frauds, and base attempts to deceive and mislead them.

Noble Massachusetts

Many men were disposed to regard these men favorably, but all sympathy was lost when they placed themselves in opposition to Massachusetts, the cradle in which the sickly puling infancy of American liberty was nursed; who has made colored men equal before her laws; who has been the protectress and benefactress of the race; who in the darkest hour of adversity, when every other State seemed bound, hand and foot, at the feet of slavery, proclaimed the right of petition against slavery; whose representatives have been insulted, abused, and their persons violated, in the halls of Congress for thundering against the citadel of Human Wrong the burnished shafts of truth and eloquence, and for her unswerving devotion to liberty, the rebel-sympathizing democracy, con-

---

come to dedicate a portion of that field as a final resting-place for those who here gave their lives that that nation might live. It is altogether fitting and proper that we should do this. But in a larger sense, we cannot dedicate, we cannot consecrate, we cannot hallow this ground. The brave men, living and dead who struggled here have consecrated it far above our poor power to add or detract. The world will little note nor long remember what we say here, but it can never forget what they did here. It is for us the living rather to be dedicated here to the unfinished work which they who fought here have thus far so nobly advanced. It is rather for us to be here dedicated to the great task remaining before us—that from these honored dead we take increased devotion to that cause for which they gave the last full measure of devotion— that we here highly resolve that these dead shall not have died in vain, that this nation under God shall have a new birth of freedom, and that government of the people, by the people, for the people shall not perish from the earth.

scious of the irresistibility of truth and justice, and that this noble old State will never furl her banner of right while a single vestige of human wrong shall disgrace the country, are now striving to reconstruct the Union, leaving her and her sister States of New England out in the cold.

Now, these men can see no potency in these claims of Massachusetts. When these facts are presented to them, they claim that we should have "State pride." I would to God that they could have heard Isaiah C. Wears's and Prof. Green's scathing rebukes to even the presumption of State pride for Pennsylvania in the breasts of colored men—a State which, instead of restoring our stolen rights, stripped us of the elective franchise, and even within the last two weeks, passed in one branch of the legislature a law excluding colored men from the State. There is no meaner State in the Union than this. She has treated the families of her soldiers worse than any other State, and with her confirmed negrophobia could we expect the treatment of dogs at her hands? But in spite of all this, if such men as J. Miller McKim, Judge Kelley, or Col. Wm. F. Small should obtain authority to raise a regiment or brigade in Pennsylvania, I would give my heart and hand to it; but knowing, as I do, that no other colored regiment will be raised in the North until the Massachusetts one is placed in the field, I say, let every man lend his influence to Massachusetts. If, by any means, the 54th should fail, it will be a blow from which we Northern men would never recover. We would be ranked with the most depraved and cowardly of men. Our enemies, infuriated as they are beyond measure, would hunt us down like so many wild beasts, while our friends, shamed and humiliated by our criminal cowardice and imbecility, would be compelled to become passive witnesses of their unbridled violence.

Look at our brethren in the South! Those who have endured all of the horrors of the Southern prisonhouse, defying the menaces of the besotted tyranny, taking up arms to achieve with their valor those rights which Providence has designed that all men should enjoy. Has freedom stultified our sterner aspirations, and made us forget our duty? Has the copperhead obtained an influence over us? If we thought that of what little freedom, we of the North enjoy, has had a tendency to nourish a disregard for our own and the rights of our fellow men, it were better that the mob-fiend drive us from off the face of the earth, to give place to those noble freedmen who are now bravely and victoriously fighting the battles of their country and liberty. We have more to gain, if victorious, or more to lose, if defeated, than any other class of men. Not abstract political rights, or religious and civil liberty, but with all these our personal liberties are to be secured. Many of us are insensible to the stern realities of the present hour, but they are here thundering at our very doors, and the sooner we awaken to their inexorable demands upon us, the better for the race, the better for the country, the better for our families, and the better for ourselves.

G.E. STEPHENS

Witness to the Draft Riots

Maria Lydig Daly

Still hard-pressed at the battlefront, the federal government passed a conscription act in the summer of 1863. The draft brought violent opposition in several Northern cities, including New York, where many people supported the cause of the secessionists. The mayor, Fernando Wood, was a well-known "Copperhead" (Confederate sympathizer) who encouraged outright insurrection against the government's conscription effort. The system of buying replacement conscripts, for the price of $300, also contributed to angry protests among workers, farmers, and others who saw the substitution system as unfairly favoring the rich.

The troubles began on Monday, July 13, 1863, the day after the names of draftees were published in local newspapers. For four days, the New York draft riots continued. By some estimates, more than one thousand persons died before the fighting, looting, and burning was finally subdued by one thousand federal troops. A New York resident, Maria Daly, recorded the events in these diary entries.

July 14, 1863

The draft began on Saturday, the eleventh, very foolishly ordered by the government, who supposed that these Union victories would make the people willing to submit. By giving them Sunday to think it over, by Monday morning there were large crowds assembled to resist the draft. All

Excerpted from Maria Lydig Daly, diary entry for July 14, 1863.

day yesterday there were dreadful scenes enacted in the city. The police were successfully opposed; many were killed, many houses were gutted and burned: the colored asylum was burned and all the furniture was carried off by *women*: Negroes were hung in the streets! All last night the fire-bells rang, but at last, in God's good mercy, the rain came down in torrents and scattered the crowds, giving the city authorities time to organize. Today bodies of police and military patrolled the city to prevent any assembly of rioters. A Virginian, last evening, harangued the crowd. Fearful that they might attack a Negro tenement house some blocks below us, as they had attacked others, I ordered the doors to be shut and no gas to be lighted in front of the house. I was afraid people would come to visit Judge Daly, ask questions, etc. I did not wonder at the spirit in which the poor resented the three hundred dollar clause.

The news from the army is most encouraging. It is thought that Lee will not be able to escape. It would seem as though the war might now be brought to an end, but this news of the riots here will give the rebels encouragement. The principal cause of discontent was the provision that by paying three hundred dollars any man could avoid serving if drafted, thus obliging all who could not beg, borrow, or steal this sum to go to the war. This is exceedingly unjust. The laboring classes say that they are sold for three hundred dollars, whilst they pay one thousand dollars for Negroes. [White draftees could pay a bounty of $300 to escape military service, while black slaves were sold for as much as $1,000.]

Things seem quiet this morning. People are returning to their homes, though the tops of the stages are crowded with workingmen and boys. . . .

Four Days of Great Anxiety

July 23, 1863

At last the riot is quelled, but we had four days of great anxiety. Fighting went on constantly in the streets between the military and police and the mob, which was partially armed. The greatest atrocities have been perpetrated.

Colonel O'Brian was murdered by the mob in such a brutal manner that nothing in the French Revolution exceeded it. Three or four Negroes were hung and burned; the women assisted and acted like furies by stimulating the men to greater ferocity. Father came into the city on Friday, being warned about his house, and found fifteen Negroes secreted in it by Rachel. They came from York Street, which the mob had attacked, with all their goods and chattels. Father had to order them out. We feared for our own block on account of the Negro tenements below MacDougal Street, where the Negroes were on the roof, singing psalms and having firearms.

One night, seeing a fire before the house, I thought the time had come, but it proved to be only a bonfire. The Judge [the author's husband] sallied out with his pistol, telling me that if he were not at home in five minutes to call up the servants. This mob seems to have a curious sense of justice. They attacked and destroyed many disreputable houses and did not always spare secessionists. On Saturday (the sixth day) we went up to see Judge Hilton, who thought me very courageous, but I felt sorry for Mrs. Hilton upon hearing that she had been so terribly frightened. She gave me such details that I came home too nervous to sleep. In Lexington Avenue, houses were destroyed. One lady before whose house the mob paused with the intention of sacking it, saved her house by raising the window, smiling, and waving her handkerchief. Mr. Bosie's brother was seized by a rioter who asked him if he had $300.

"No," said he.

"Then come along with us," said the rioter, and they kept him two hours. Mrs. Hilton said she never saw such creatures, such gaunt-looking savage men and women and even little children armed with brickbats, stones, pokers, shovels and tongs, coal-scuttles, and even tin pans and bits of iron. They passed her house about four o'clock on Monday morning and continued on in a constant stream until nine o'clock. They looked to her, she said, like Germans, and her first thought was that it was some German festival. Whilst we sat there, we heard occasional pistol shots, and I was very glad that I had ordered a carriage to take us home. The carriage, it seems, was very unwillingly sent since the livery-stable keeper was so much afraid.

Every evening the Judge *would* go out near eleven o'clock, to my great distress. But he threatened to send me into the country if I objected (which I dreaded still more), so I kept quiet. (James) Leonard, the Superintendent of Police in our neighborhood, said the draft could not be enforced; the firemen are against it, as well as all the working classes.

Among those killed or wounded have been found men with delicate hands and feet, and under their outward laborers' clothes were fine cambric shirts and costly underclothing. [Gentlemen were disguising themselves as laborers in order to riot anonymously.] A dressmaker says she saw from her window a gentleman whom she knows and has seen with young ladies, but whose name she could not remember, disguised in this way in the mob on Sixth Avenue.

On Sunday we went to see Mrs. (Nathaniel) Jarvis and Mr. James T. Brady, who had just arrived from Washington. I saw Susanna Brady, who talked in the most violent manner against the Irish and in favor of the blacks. I feel quite differently, although very sorry and much outraged at the cruelties inflicted. I hope it will give the Negroes a lesson, for since the war commenced, they have been so insolent as to be unbearable. I cannot endure free blacks. They are immoral, with all their piety.

A Secessionist Plot

The principal actors in this mob were boys, and I think they were Americans. Catherine, my seamstress, tells me that the plundering was done by the people in the neighborhood who were looking on and who, as the mob broke the houses open, went in to steal. The police this morning found beds, bedding, and furniture in the house of a Scotch Presbyterian who was well off and owned two cows and two horses. The Catholic priests have done their duty as Christian ministers in denouncing these riotous proceedings. One of them remonstrated with a woman in the crowd who wanted to cut off the ears of a Negro (who) was hung. The priest told her that Negroes had souls, "Sure, your reverence," said she, "I thought they only had gizzards."

On Sunday evening, Mr. Dykes came in. He had seen Judge Pierrepont, who had gone to Washington with others to see what can be done. Mr. Dykes thinks that New York, being a Democratic city, may expect little indulgence from the Administration. The Judge went up to see General Dix, now in command here, who says that the government is determined to carry the draft measure through at all costs. Yesterday we went to the wedding of Lydia Watson in Westchester County. Mr. (James) Adie told the Judge that there was a secessionist plot to burn all the houses in the neighborhood on Thursday night, that he had heard that his had been exempted by vote, and the principal instigator and mover in it was one of the richest and most influential men in the neighborhood. The purpose of the plot was to intimidate the government and prevent conscription. Mrs. Harry Morris, who I hear has been very violent in her invectives against the North, wished to know if the soldiers could be relied upon. I told her entirely so, that they declared they would rather fight these traitors at home who made this fire in their rear whilst they were risking their life to preserve order and the laws than the rebels. For her comfort, I told her that the mob had destroyed the houses of secessionists. I frightened her, I think, not a little.

The Advantages of Slavery

John Bell Robinson

The argument over slavery and secession, abolition and states' rights, burned just as hot among Northerners as it did between the people of North and South. In the principal cities of the North, newspaper editors fought long, violent campaigns in their columns, politicians debated the questions endlessly in city halls and state legislatures, and church ministers attacked their ideological foes with the weapons of Biblical quotation and Christian theology. Philadelphia, the "City of Brotherly Love," set the scene for bitter accusations and feuding among the leaders of the Methodist Episcopal Church, which divided in 1844 on the question of slavery and deposed its leader, a bishop who had married a slave-owning woman. This incident angered and inspired John Bell Robinson to collect sermons, letters, and articles into *Pictures of Slavery and Anti-Slavery,* published in the midst of the war in 1863.

Robinson's arguments were familiar to his readers: the slaves were happier as slaves than they ever would be as free individuals; the emancipation of the slaves would bring about social chaos within the United States; the dissolution of the Union was too high a price to pay for the opinions and causes of fanatic Northern abolitionists, who, secretly, were determined to undermine the United States as well as its foundation as a Christian nation. In his article, *Who are Union Men?,* Robinson also makes a telling point against the Northern anti-slavery faction: The same abolitionists who had brought about the Civil War were raising not a whisper of

Excerpted from John Bell Robinson, *Pictures of Slavery and Anti-Slavery* (Philadelphia: n.p., 1863).

protest over a tragedy just as terrible and unjust as slavery: the destruction of the original Native American inhabitants of the continent and the theft of their land.

I meet with men every day who cry loudly for the Union, and urge the prosecution of the war beyond possibility; and denounce the administration, Gen. Winfield Scott, and Gen. George McClellan [generals who commanded Northern armies at the start of the war], for not having pushed the war on before this, to the total destruction of the whole South, with their entire interest, without the slightest respect to the helpless women and children. They seem to be so aggrieved and mortified at the Southern people for attempting to destroy this great and glorious Union, that many of them say that the whole white population of the seceding States must be exterminated for the crime they have committed in the attempt to withdraw from the Union. They most bitterly denounce every man as a traitor who speaks of trying to save the Union without the destruction of human life. *Yet they say they never want to see the Union restored with peace and harmony, while there is a slave on American soil. No! rather than have one negro in slavery in the United States, they would see the Union split into fragments, and a monarchical government established with the most extreme despotism ever known.* Or rather than yield up one single line of the Chicago Platform [program of the 1860 Republican party, which condoned slavery], or to allow one single slave to go into the territories of the United States under protection of law, or one sent back to his master who had made his escape into the free States, " let the Constitution slide," let the Union be broken up, let anarchy reign from Maine to Florida, and from the Atlantic to the Pacific. This class of men, and women too, are very large in this city of Brotherly Love [Philadelphia], and they allow no man to speak of peace through the medium of olive-branches. If he dare do it, they denounce him as a secessionist, and tell him he ought to be hung upon the lamp-post by the neck, or locked up in a prison cell and kept there until he rots. One of these kind of Union men, a large merchant in this city, said he had two sons in the battle field, and if he had forty, he would send them all to save this glorious Union from destruction, and if one refused to go he would disown him. Yet this great patriot denounces the Constitution as a compromise with the devil and a league with hell. There are thousands upon thousands of these great patriotic Union men who would rather anything should take place, no matter how devilish, than there should be one single negro slave in the United States.

"Wolves in Sheep's Clothing"

Now, I cannot conceive of but one way to solve this enigma, and that is as follows: In the first place they are "wolves in sheep's clothing," as set forth in the Bible. Secondly, they are servants of old Apollyon [anti-Christian pagans], and hate Christianity, and all that is good in this world; in short, they are an infidel crew, sent forth by the father of lies and the hater of God and all good government, to destroy this model government, simply because it was marked out by the finger of *Jehovah,* and destined to remodel the whole world, and usher in the *millennium* spoken of in the Scriptures. It would not be hard to prove that the great love and sympathy they profess to feel for the poor slave is a false pretext, feigned for the purpose of breaking up the Union between the North and South, and not that they care anything about the poor Africans in slavery, or have the slightest conscientious scruples on the subject of slavery or slaveholding. But they hate pure Christianity more than they love the Constitution, therefore their opposition to Southern slavery. Why? Because they know there is no other sectional question of interest in the United States, and they know that to be a vital and exciting one to the Southern people. If there were no slaves they would seize upon something else the most exciting in the country. If these people have so much sympathy for the poor negro, how is it they have none for any other species of mankind? Every man or woman who has any knowledge of facts in the case, knows the slaves to be well off, and a great deal better off than one-half of the white population of the free States. They have few or no troubles, and are the happiest people on earth; they have no concern beyond the present moment. Then why is it there is so much concern felt for the poor slaves, while the free people of color are in so much worse condition in every shape and form, and no sympathy felt or expressed for them whatever?

Where Are the Indians?

Where are the thousands of Indians who occupied the very ground on which this great city is built? They pre-occupied this soil, and in that way were the rightful owners of every foot of earth now occupied in the United States by the white man. But where are they to-day? Have they not been driven from their rights and rightful homes, to the western wilds and Rocky Mountains, and thousands upon thousands of them murdered and slaughtered in their own homes, simply because they contended for their birthright? Millions of them have been compelled to perish with cold and hunger, under the snow-flakes of the Rocky Mountains, after having been driven from their just rights and happy homes. Who will pretend to say this is not real robbery, theft, and murder? But who has condemned all this wickedness? Where are the long aping and pitiful faces that have been forced or feigned, or those that originated from pure sympathy, to be found among all the sympathizers in this country with the poor slaves, who have every right conceded to them they ever bad or now have? They are well clad and fed, cared for and respected, and enjoy all the fruits of their labor, even more than Stephen Girard [a wealthy Philadelphia philanthropist] ever did. They have good homes, the doctor when sick, and are well nursed. There is not one to be found in the United States, who owes one cent, and all who do right are as happy as men can be in this world of sin. Yet this great and glorious Union which has produced such happiness and peace to the Africans, is to be broken up, and the whole white population reduced to slavery, under some despotic monarch or thrown into a state of anarchy, rather than one negro should be left in slavery in the United States, the only condition of peace and safety they ever will find in this world.

A Divisive Question

Now tell me how is this, that we must give up all that is dear to us in this world, and not do the slaves any good, but reduce them to a far worse condition than their present one, and not even a complaint made against the treatment to the poor Indians, who have been robbed of all their rights, and slain like blackbirds, and driven back to the very ends of the earth, and there left to perish! For all this, not one association formed, or a meeting called, or a tear dropped, nor no long sympathetic aping faces made by those who would give up all that is good, rather than there should be one negro left in slavery in this great country. I will tell you how it is. The Indian question cannot be made a sectional one. The whole country is of the same opinion, and it would produce no opposition between the North and South, nor the East and West. It would rather tend to strengthen the Union, therefore it would not answer the purpose. But the slave question is a sectional one, it strikes at the very vitals of the benefits of one-half of the soil of this country, the dearest rights of the people thereof, and the Constitution of the United States. It aims a death blow at all the civil, social, and domestic institutions of all the States. And all this is aimed at the very vitals of this great Union. It is done because the Union encourages Christianity through the Gospel of Christ. If I am wrong I hope some one will set me right. Ask those men what they propose to do with five millions of free negroes suddenly turned loose on the country! Some answer that they will leave that for an after consideration; others say that they have nothing to do with it, that their business is to free them; and some say they may go to the devil for all they care about them; but others say they must be placed on an equality, that our Creator had made us all equal, therefore we are compelled to take them into a political, social, and domestic equality. Mr. G., who is rather a fine-looking man, said to me the other day, in the presence of a number of witnesses, that he was no respecter of persons on account of their color, that he would just as soon take the arm, of a black person, or have them take his *(male or female of course)* and walk through the city, or promenade the social circle, *as he would a white person.* Mr. G. is well-known in this city. A large majority of the above named Union men are of this class, according to their declarations.

The Total Destruction of the Union

Now, I don't believe one word of such asseverations, nor do I believe any man of common sense or good judgment does; for such a thing is contrary to human nature and common sense. All such asseverations are for effect, and all such persons would be the first to rebel against any government that would attempt to enforce it, even if it was the government of *Jehovah himself,* if it was made morally and civilly right to do so. All such declarations are without the slightest foundation in honest truth, and have an ulterior object in view, and that is the total destruction of this great and glorious Union. They are the very men who have brought us to this awful crisis, and now denounce every man as a secessionist who dares to speak of saving the Union, and restoring peace, tranquillity, and harmony, in any other way than the one that will eternally destroy it, just as sure as we have had peace and prosperity through and by the Constitution and the Union. Yea! as sure as there is a heaven above and an earth beneath, our peace and harmony is gone, eternally gone, if the above class of Union men are allowed to lead or are listened to. They know well that a free republican Union cannot exist with five millions of inhabitants interspersed among them totally incapable of self-government or of being made so. And even if they were, human nature is such that they could not be admitted on an equality, for which they would sue in less than five years. Then a scene would transpire such as the sun has never shone upon. Our soil would be drenched with human gore from one end to the other; and our Union that has been the harbinger of peace, love, tranquillity, and harmony would suddenly be convert-

Freed slaves are shown at a village in Arlington, Virginia. Some Northerners argued that the destruction of the Union was too high a price to pay for ending slavery in the South.

ed into a reign of anarchy, which would exist as long as there was a colored person on American soil, or a terrible despotism established by some tyrant of a Nero [Roman emperor who ruled from A.D. 54–68], who would seize the reins of government, mount the throne, and reduce us all to slavery, or to an equality without the slightest respect to color, and that would be the end of civil and religious liberty. I look upon this class of fanatics as being just such as the devil would have them to be.

Slavery Safeguards the Free Black Man

I will say, in conclusion, that, as long as the slaves are let alone, in the possession of their masters, the free people of color will be safe in this country, and their rights cared for, but no longer. The four and a half millions of slaves in the United States are the only safeguards the free black man has, and none would suffer a greater overthrow by the emancipation of all the slaves, or destruction of the Union, than they. In either case, they will be the greater losers, unless a Nero should seize the reins of government at the same time, with five hundred thousand troops under his control. This would end all controversy, and forever solve the question of the capability of man for self-government.

Chapter 6

Doctoring for the North

Chapter Preface

The Medical Department of the United States Army, much like the rest of the military service, was caught unprepared at the start of the Civil War. Under its aging leader, Thomas Lawson, the department was understaffed, undersupplied, and barely capable of tending to the needs of the army in peacetime. At the war's beginning, fewer than 100 doctors were employed, and the department was short of medical instruments, medicines, even thermometers and bandages. The shortage of trained doctors worsened when more than one-quarter joined the Confederate army or fled to private practice. State examining boards, faced with the need to certify their replacements, passed poorly trained and sometimes completely unqualified candidates in order to fill the quota demanded of each state.

Once they were accepted into service, the army doctors realized they would be dealing with much more than gunshot or bayonet wounds. The primitive and unsanitary conditions in the army camps caused epidemics of diseases, such as chicken pox, mumps, and measles, often even before the troops were mustered to the front. Once reaching the field, soldiers were exposed to contaminated water, inadequate shelter, and a poor diet, leading to epidemics of dysentery, typhoid, diphtheria, tuberculosis, pneumonia, malaria, yellow fever, and cholera.

Battles turned the field hospitals into hellish scenes of carnage and death. The majority of wounds were caused by the new minié ball, a conical lead bullet that tore through flesh and bone, causing heavy bleeding and shock. Wounds to arms and legs often required amputation, as there were no medications available to prevent gangrene. Patients had to endure the procedure with the comfort of a shot of whiskey, a chloroform-soaked rag pressed over the mouth, or no anesthetic at all. A bullet wound to the abdomen, where infection spread rapidly from the perforated stomach or intestines, meant almost certain death.

Despite the hardships, the doctors and nurses of the Union army's medical corps remained dedicated to the cause of saving lives and serving the Union. Theirs are some of the most compelling tales ever told of the Civil War experience.

A Volunteer Surgeon Marches with General Grant

John G. Perry

In 1862, facing a shortage of doctors, the federal government called for volunteer surgeons to serve in military hospitals behind the lines in order to allow commissioned army surgeons to remain at the battlefronts. John Perry, a student at the Boston Medical School, answered the government's call. Perry hoped that his wartime experience would allow him to take his final examinations sooner—a feat which would also allow him to marry his fiancee, Martha Derby.

Perry was assigned to the Army of the Potomac under General Ulysses S. Grant in the spring of 1864. Grant's forces were force-marched through eastern Virginia, and Perry witnessed some of the worst fighting of the entire war at the battles of The Wilderness, Spotsylvania Courthouse, Cold Harbor, and Petersburg. His letters home to the future Martha Derby Perry reveal a caring and competent surgeon overwhelmed by the carnage and suffering he witnessed during this campaign.

Banks of the Mattapony River
May 22nd, 1864

It has rained every day for a week; the mud is several feet deep, and the men thoroughly waterlogged, but nevertheless, they are cheerful and ready to begin the contest again. I dread the results of a fight, but must confess, as it seems

Excerpted from *Letters from a Surgeon of the Civil War*, by John G. Perry as compiled by Martha Derby Perry (Boston: Little, Brown, 1906).

the only way of forcing the end, I want to go ahead.

We are not allowed mail facilities in this campaign, and our only opportunities for sending letters North are by the wounded on their way to the rear. I have material enough for fifty letters, but dare not risk it in the hands of wounded privates.

Our corps, the Second, is separated from the main army. We made a forced march to this place, which is called Milford, night before last and yesterday. We are two miles from Bowling Green, by the Fredericksburg and Richmond Railroad, and on the banks of the Mattapony River. General Hancock made this move successfully, but with a loss of about fifty of his cavalry. This is the route by which General Lee sent all his wounded to Richmond. We are almost directly in General Lee's rear,—at any rate, so far in his rear that it is probable he will have to fall back in order to fight us. We have entrenched ourselves as securely as we can, and the river covers both our flanks. The Second corps is estimated at twenty-five thousand men.

On one of the recent days of fighting, at early dawn the troops were in line, when the order was given to charge without noise. While on the run,—I following with my hospital steward about twenty yards in the rear of the men,— we saw in a clump of bushes a pair of boots with the soles up, as if the owner had taken a headlong leap into the hedge. Stopping to investigate, I pulled out Captain Kelliher of the Twentieth. He was horribly mangled about the face and neck, as if from a shell or solid shot; yet no gun had been heard, and no one seen to leave the ranks.

I found him bleeding freely from a laceration of the subclavian artery, showing that the injury could only have been received a moment before, else he would have bled to death. He was still living, though unconscious, and after tying the artery, so as to stop the hemorrhage, he was placed on a stretcher and carried to the rear. The fighting lasted but a short time; as the Confederates were but partially surprised, they rallied and held us in check.

As soon as the Division Hospital tents were up, I had Kelliher taken to Dr. Hayward, who, finding him still alive, though yet unconscious, decided to remove the shattered bones and to clean and stitch the wounds, so as to give him all the comfort possible, but with no hope of saving his life. Under the chloroform the captain rallied still more, and a few hours after our work was finished he finally became conscious. Dr. Hayward had removed the shattered lower jaw, the whole arm, including a shoulder-blade, or scapula, the clavicle or collarbone, and a large part of the first two ribs on the same side of the body, as all these broken bones were lacerating the flesh, and the surfaces of the lung were exposed. When the operation was completed, the line of suture for closing the wounds ran from the ear to within an inch or two of the pelvis.

I placed the patient under my shelter tent, and ordered the steward to feed and stimulate him as directed. In the night it rained so hard that I dug a trench about him to keep him from being drenched and chilled. The following day we were ordered to push on, and to place the wounded, who were unable to march, in army wagons destined for the "White House Landing," which was twenty miles away. What was to become of poor Kelliher? Surely he could never survive such a strain, even though at the time he was doing well. After much deliberation I decided to consult the captain himself, and to follow his decision. In presenting to him the situation, I offered to remain with him in case he wished to be left, and told him that we must simply make up our minds to be captured by the enemy; but his answer was clear and prompt: "I will go to the White House Landing, Doctor, and, Doctor, I *shall* live." So, doing what was possible to make him comfortable with the use of straw and grass by way of a mattress, I bade him good-bye, never dreaming that he could survive such a journey.[*]

Two Miles from Hanover Junction
May 24th, 1864
I can scratch only a few lines, being up to my elbows in

* (Original author's note) Captain Kelliher, after complete recovery rejoined the Twentieth and was commissioned its major, and remained in active service with the regiment till the end of the war.

blood. Oh, the fatigue and endless work we surgeons have! About one night in three to sleep in, and then we are so nervous and played out that sleep is impossible.

The hospital is fast filling up with poor fellows who last night charged upon the enemy's works on the other side of the river. We are some fifteen miles nearer Richmond than when I last wrote, and the strongest works of the Confederacy are at this point and at the South Anna River. They were thrown up during the first year of the war.

It looks now as if we should still compel the enemy to fall back. We have had a deal of forced marching lately, and the heat has been almost intolerable. At times it has seemed as if the sun's rays would lay us out, yet we march all day, and through volumes upon volumes of dense dust. News has just come that the Confederates are falling back, and so I suppose we must pack our wounded into wagons and move after them with all the speed possible.

It seems to me I am quite callous to death now, and that I could see my dearest friend die without much feeling. This condition tells a long story which, under other circumstances, could scarcely be imagined. During the last three weeks I have seen probably no less than two thousand deaths, and among them those of many dear friends. I have witnessed hundreds of men shot dead, have walked and slept among them, and surely I feel it possible to die myself as calmly as any,—but enough of this. The fight is now fearful, and ambulances are coming in with great rapidity, each bearing its suffering load.

Fourteen Miles from White House on York River
May 30th, 1864

We are now fourteen miles from Richmond, having marched pretty steadily southward ever since I last wrote. Oh, why will not the Confederacy burst up! True, we are drawing very near to Richmond, but the tug of war will come at the Chickahominy River. Although the Confederates had the shortest road, we rather stole a march upon them this time before they could reach and stop us, and, by making a hard, forced march, we saved many lives. The morale of the enemy is injured by their falling back in retreat so far, while that of our army is correspondingly improved. They are now pretty near their last ditch, and the fight there will be fierce and strong. I work day and night, and when not busy with the sick and wounded am on the tedious march.

Cold Harbor
June 4th, 1864

I have not had a moment to write for nearly a week. It has been fight, fight, fight. Every day there is a fight, and every day the hospital is again filled. For four days now we have been operating upon the men wounded in one battle, which lasted only about two hours; but the wounds were more serious than those from former engagements. I am heartsick over it all. If the Confederates lost in each fight the same number as we, there would be more chance for us; but their loss is about one man to our five, from the fact that they never leave their earthworks, whereas our men are obliged to charge even when there is not the slightest chance of taking them. Several times after capturing these works our troops were unsupported and had to evacuate immediately, with great loss. The men are becoming discouraged, but there is plenty of fight in them yet.

June 7th, 1864

For the first time, I believe, since this campaign commenced, I am lying upon my blankets at twelve o'clock noon. This morning early we sent almost every man in the hospital to the "White House," to make room for others. Under a flag of truce, we asked permission of the enemy to take off our wounded who were lying between the two lines. This, of course, prevented all hostilities, and we surgeons are having a few hours' rest.

June 10th, 1864

The front lines are within thirty yards of the Confederate works,—indeed, so near that a biscuit could easily be tossed into them. On neither side do the men dare show their heads above the entrenchments, for it is almost sure death to do so. The sharpshooters on both sides are so placed that they can pick off anything which appears in sight.

We have had thirty of our division wounded to-day by shell which the Confederates manage to throw into our pits, but we are successful in dropping some into theirs also. The heat is intolerable, and the roads are covered with dust six or eight inches deep, which every gust of wind sweeps up, covering everything with a dirty, white coating.

Field Hospital near Petersburg
June 24th, 1864

I am up to my neck in work. It is slaughter, slaughter. Our brigade has met with a sad loss by having three entire regiments gobbled up as prisoners. The Twentieth fortunately escaped. This misfortune was caused by the second brigade giving way before the attack of the enemy and exposing the flank of our own. The enemy, before we knew it, was in our rear, and resistance was absurd. Major Hooper, who commanded the brigade, was the only one of the Fifteenth Massachusetts who escaped. He received a slight wound in the arm, however, and started for home yesterday. Lucky fellow! No time for writing more.

June 27th, 1864

When our division was withdrawn from the extreme front, where it has been since the beginning of the campaign, we surgeons looked for a little less arduous work; but now the artillery brigade has been placed under our care, and we have as much to do as ever. It has not rained for a month, and the poor wounded fellows lie all about me, suffering intensely from heat and flies. The atmosphere is almost intolerable from the immense quantity of decomposing animal and vegetable matter upon the ground. Many of the surgeons are ill, and I indulge in large doses of quinine. Horses and mules die by hundreds from continued hard labor and scant feed. The roads are strew with them, and the decay of these, with that of human bodies in the trenches, causes malaria of the worst kind.

War! War! War! I often think that in the future when human character shall have deepened, there will be a better way of settling affairs than this of plunging into a perfect maelstrom of horror.

Life on a Hospital Cot

Robert Hale Strong

Union officers as well as enlisted men feared the army hospital as much as, and sometimes more than, the fighting on the battlefield. Civil War hospitals were well known among the soldiers for their unsanitary conditions and for their fearful scenes of pain, injury, and death. In fact, more men died from disease and the complications brought on by surgery performed under primitive conditions than died on the battlefield. The hospital also separated the soldiers from their units, a source of shame and worry as regimental comrades were left behind at the front lines to carry on the fight. In the summer of 1864, Private Robert Strong took sick while marching in Georgia with his regiment. He was ordered to a field hospital just before the Battle of Marietta, then sent back to a Union base hospital in Chattanooga, Tennessee. The following is his account of hospital conditions.

About the sixth day of July, 1864, I got so bad with rheumatism and dysentery that I could not walk. I went and lay down under the doctor's tent. We were then near Marietta. On the morning that the regiment marched on to Marietta, I was a little in the rear when the bugles sounded. "Fall in!" I picked up my gun and started to go to the regiment. When I got part way, I fell down beside a tree.

The colonel passed and saw me. He asked what I was doing there and why I was not in a hospital. I told him I did

Excerpted from *A Yankee Private's Civil War*, by Robert Hale Strong (Chicago: Regnery, 1961).

not want to go to the hospital, so had started for the regiment. He ordered me to stay where I was while he sent for
our doctor. Before he came, Doctor Beggs, who belonged to
us but had been detailed to a New Jersey regiment, came
along, saw me, and had me taken by ambulance to the division hospital in the rear. This was a temporary tent affair.

That night, the boys came to see me. They said the
colonel just raised h— with our doctor for not taking better
care of the boys, and asked why he had not sent me to the
hospital where I belonged.

After the Battle of Marietta, the hospital soon filled with
wounded and sick. The hospital doctor came through to decide who among us should be sent farther to the rear. No
real soldier wanted to go to the hospital. We were all lying
on the ground, so as soon as I saw the doctor coming, I sat
up. I tried to make him think I was able to go to the front,
but he ordered me to get ready to go back to Chattanooga.
It did not take me long to get ready, as my wardrobe was all
on my back and feet.

When the ambulance came for us, we were taken to the
railroad cars. These were cattle cars, with a little straw on
the bottom. We had to pack close to get into them. None of
us were able to stand or sit up many minutes at a time and
the hospital men who were with us to help us could not do
much for us except bring water.

So many trains were rushing to the front with rations and
ammunition that our progress was slow. We took three days
getting to Chattanooga. While on the train, I traded coffee
and sugar—I had been too sick to eat for a long time and
had several pounds of each—for blackberries. I got my
haversack, cup, and cap full. I ate them all and traded for
more. In those three days I think I ate a bushel of berries,
and I have always believed that they saved my life.

At the Chattanooga Hospital

Ambulances met the train at Chattanooga and took us to the
hospital. Each man had a narrow cot with a clean sheet. The
first thing I remember in the hospital was sitting up on my

cot and pulling my shirt over my head. The male nurse spoke pleasantly to me, and said I had better keep my shirt on. He told me afterwards that I had been crazy for three days and that if I had not been so weak they would have had to tie me down. Said I had eaten nothing since I arrived there.

The nurse then asked my name, company and regiment; what state I was from; my father's and mother's names and where they lived. He wrote it all down on a piece of paper and fastened it to the head of my bed. I asked him, "What's all that for?" and he said, so that if I died, they could notify my regiment and my people. I remember telling him I did not propose to die yet. He laughed and said, "So?" and nothing more.

Everyone was very kind and good to the very sick who were expected to get well, but those who seemed nearly dead had little attention paid to them except to see that they received what they needed. There had been a big battle at the front and soon the wounded were brought in.

After my talk with the nurse, the next thing I remember is seeing a young and handsome boy, who lay next to me on the right, keep picking at his fingers and then at his nose. I spoke to him, but he paid no attention to me. Soon the doctor came, examined me, added a little to the card the nurse had put up, and then went to the boy.

I then learned why the boy did not answer me. He did not know anything. He had been shot clear through the head, the ball entering just under the eye and coming out at the back of his head. The doctor took a silk rag, oiled it, threaded it into a long silver needle, and pushed the needle clear through the boy's head. He drew the silk rag after it and brought out three or four great big maggots. He repeated this several times, all the while talking soothingly to the boy. Then he dressed the wound and gave the boy something to quiet his nerves.

The next man had been shot through the body. The doctor with his probe went into the wound, cleaned it, pushed some cotton into the wound to keep it open, and went on.

By this time I was sick of it. My stomach had nothing in it,

The Civil War Medicine Chest

During the Civil War, hard-pressed doctors tried a variety of new and untested methods and materials to care for the sick and wounded. In What They Didn't Teach You About the Civil War, *Mike Wright recounts some of the war's medical malpractice.*

North and South, alcohol was the most commonly used drug, not as an antiseptic, since doctors knew nothing of sepsis, but as whiskey. It was often given to wounded soldiers taken to field stations after a battle. The idea was to prevent shock. It wasn't exactly successful, but it was a very popular remedy among the troops.

There were, of course, other remedies. In 1861, a committee of New York City hospital physicians prepared a *Manual of Directions* for use in Union army hospitals. It offered *Drinks for the sick* (toast water, apple tea, rice water, and plain lemonade), proposed *Articles of diet for the sick* (egg brandy, milk punch, sago posset, and oatmeal gruel), and suggested *External applications* (water and vapor baths, poultices). There was even something known as "evaporating lotions."

Cold water, spirit and water, equal parts; a solution of muriate of ammonia, a dram to the pint; a solution of sugar of lead and opium, a half dram of each to the pint of hot water, are frequently ordered as lotions. They are to be applied by means of a single layer of muslin or linen, which is to be kept constantly moist with the lotion.

The manual suggested using blisters, leeches, and enemas, the last said to be "injections . . . intended to be either purgative, sedative, or nutritious." It prescribed opium with no hesitation but suggested, in the making of wine whey (goat's milk and wine), that in this "and all other articles containing alcoholic stimulants, specific directions should be obtained from the medical attendant, as to the proportion of wine or spirits to be used. . . ."

Mike Wright, *What They Didn't Teach You About the Civil War.* Novato, CA: Presidio, 1996.

or it would have come up. Before this, I had seen men killed by the hundred and cut to pieces by shells. But I had never seen a doctor cut a man up. I surely did while I was there.

The Amputating Room

At the end of our tent, separated from us only by a flap of cloth, was the amputating room. I, being near the end, could hear and see nearly everything done there.

As soon as possible, they placed men from the same commands together. In a few days they put near me two of my regiment, one wounded in the leg and the other in the arm. Both had to have their limbs amputated. First they took to the table a boy from near Downer's Grove named Depew or something like it. They carried Depew over while the others were asleep. They took his wounded arm off and took him back. He never opened his mouth during the operation, but he looked mighty pale when they brought him back. As soon as they laid him on his cot, he grasped my hand with the one he had left, but he did not cry.

When they took the other man out, he began to curse and cry. All the chloroform they gave him did not quiet his tongue, and he kept yelling and cursing and crying, "Oh!" all the time that they were cutting off his leg, even though the chloroform held his leg still.

In a few days, both the amputees and the boy with the hole through his head were sent to Nashville, as that place was farther from the front and all hospitals here were filled up again as fast as they were emptied. Two kinds of patients stayed—those who could not recover, and those who would soon be ready to go back to duty at the front. . . .

Getting Well

During this time, our hospital food was what we called soft diet. It consisted mostly of soups and soft bread with butter, jellies, jams. As we grew stronger, they gave us mashed potatoes and a small piece of beef steak. Each boy's meal was brought to him on a tray and set on his bed. If he was too weak to feed himself, he was fed and coaxed to eat.

Some had a ravenous appetite which had almost to be choked off. Others wanted nothing. The nurses would coax them, "Eat a little so you'll be able to go home on furlough."

When I got well enough to go outdoors, I had my first good chance to see the outside of a big army hospital. I found the hospital was laid off in streets. Each street was numbered, and every eight or ten tents were called a ward. I was in Ward B, I forget the street number.

In the adjoining tent were some desperately wounded men. One day the sergeant in charge of our ward asked me to go to the next tent with him to see them dress the wounds of a certain badly wounded man. This man was hit in the left side. The shell had cut away a portion of his side, ribs and all. When his wound was exposed for dressing, one could see his heart beat. I did not learn whether he ever recovered, but they were doing their best for him.

Another fellow in the same tent was badly wounded but in a very awkward way. He had lost so big a piece of flesh, behind, that he could not sit down. If he recovered, a bustle would become him.

Eighteen or twenty rods from my tent, and just in front of it, was the "Dead House." All bodies were taken directly from the wards to the Dead House, and if not claimed and removed by friends, they were cut up. There were always many citizen doctors present there from pure patriotism and for the chance they had of dissecting the dead. All remains were supposed to be given honorable burial after dissection, but I suppose those in charge of the burials found their sad work confusing. Sometimes, I know, they did not do their job. The hospital privies were next to the Dead House. Many times, I have seen the intestines of dead men in the vault. More than once, I have seen the intestines hanging from the seats, not having been pushed in properly. It was horrible, but we got used to it. And all the while, we knew we would be misused the same way if we died. A live man was taken care of, but a dead man was no good except to experiment with.

Tending to the Sick

Walt Whitman

Already known for his volumes of poetry, including *Leaves of Grass,* writer Walt Whitman volunteered for service as a hospital nurse in Washington, D.C. In the nation's capital he discovered that more than 50 hospitals and convalescent camps had been set up in wooden barracks, public buildings, and within vast tents, some of them covering entire city blocks. Moved by the many stories of individual suffering and sacrifice, he set down his thoughts in letters, in diary entries, and in regular dispatches to newspapers back home in New York. The following dispatch describes Whitman's encounter with a young and deathly ill soldier from Plymouth, Massachusetts, and reveals how the writer's care and sympathy saved a life.

*D*ispatch to the New York Times, *February 26, 1863.* The military hospitals, convalescent camps, etc. in Washington and its neighborhood sometimes contain over fifty thousand sick and wounded men. Every form of wound (the mere sight of some of them having been known to make a tolerably hardy visitor faint away), every kind of malady— like a long procession, with typhoid, and diarrhoea at the head as leaders—are here in steady motion. The soldiers' hospital! How many sleepless nights, how many women's tears, how many long and waking hours and days of suspense from every one of the Middle, Eastern, and Western states have concentrated here! Our own New York, in the form of hundreds and thousands of her young men, may consider herself here; Pennsylvania, Ohio, Indiana, and all

Excerpted from Walt Whitman's dispatch to the *New York Times*, February 26, 1863.

the West and Northwest the same, and all the New England States the same!

Upon a few of these hospitals I have been almost daily calling on a mission, on my own account, for the sustenance and consolation of some of the most needy cases of sick and dying men for the last two months. One has much to learn to do good in these places. Great tact is required. These are not like other hospitals. By far the greatest proportion (I should say five sixths) of the patients are American young men, intelligent, of independent spirit, tender feelings, used to a hardy and healthy life; largely the farmers are represented by their sons—largely the mechanics and working-men of the cities. Then they are soldiers. All these points must be borne in mind. . . .

Used with Great Indifference

Of course, there are among these thousands of prostrated soldiers in hospital here all sorts of individual cases. On recurring to my notebook, I am puzzled which cases to select to illustrate the average of these young men and their experiences. I may say here, too, in general terms, that I could not wish for more candor and manliness among all their sufferings than I find among them.

Take this case in Ward 6, Campbell Hospital, a young man from Plymouth County, Massachusetts; a farmer's son, aged about twenty or twenty-one—a soldierly, American young fellow, but with sensitive and tender feelings. Most of December and January last he lay very low, and for quite a while I never expected he would recover. He had become prostrated with an obstinate diarrhoea; his stomach would hardly keep the least thing down; he was vomiting half the time. But that was hardly the worst of it. Let me tell you his story—it is but one of thousands.

He had been some time sick with his regiment in the field, in front, but did his duty as long as he could; was in the battle of Fredericksburg; soon after was put in the regimental hospital. He kept getting worse—could not eat anything they had there; the doctor told him nothing could be done for him there. The poor fellow had fever also; received (perhaps it could not be helped) little or no attention; lay on the ground getting worse. Toward the latter part of December, very much enfeebled, he was sent up from the front, from Falmouth Station, in an open platform car (such as hogs are transported upon North), and dumped with a crowd of others on the boat at Aquia Creek, falling down like a rag where they deposited him, too weak and sick to sit up or help himself at all. No one spoke to him or assisted him; he had nothing to eat or drink; was used (amid the great crowds of sick) with perfect indifference, or, as in two or three instances, with heartless brutality.

On the boat, when night came and when the air grew chilly, he tried a long time to undo the blankets he had in his knapsack, but was too feeble. He asked one of the employees who was moving around deck for a moment's assistance to get the blankets. The man asked him back if he could not get them himself. He answered, no, he had been trying for more than half an hour and found himself too weak. The man rejoined he might then go without them, and walked off. So H. lay chilled and damp on deck all night, without anything under or over him, while two good blankets were within reach. It caused him a great injury, nearly cost him his life.

Life and Near Death in Ward 6

Arrived at Washington, he was brought ashore and again left on the wharf or above it, amid the great crowds, as before, without any nourishment, not a drink for his parched mouth; no kind hand had offered to cover his face from the forenoon sun. Conveyed at last some two miles by the ambulance to the hospital and assigned a bed (Bed 49, Campbell Hospital, January and February, 1863), he fell down exhausted upon the bed. But the ward-master (he has since been changed) came to him with a growling order to get up; the rules, he said, permitted no man to lie down in that way with his own clothes on; he must sit up—must first go to the bathroom, be washed, and have his clothes properly changed. (A very good

Wounded soldiers receive medical attention at one of the many hospitals and convalescent camps set up for their care in Washington, D.C.

rule, properly applied.) He was taken to the bathroom and scrubbed well with cold water. The attendants, callous for a while, were soon alarmed, for suddenly the half-frozen and lifeless body fell limpsy in their hands, and they hurried it back to the cot, plainly insensible, perhaps dying.

Poor boy! The long train of exhaustion, deprivation, rudeness, no food, no friendly word or deed, but all kinds of upstart airs and impudent, unfeeling speeches and deeds from all kinds of small officials (and some big ones), cutting like razors into that sensitive heart, had at last done the job. He now lay, at times out of his head but quite silent, asking nothing of anyone for some days, with death getting a closer and a surer grip upon him; he cared not, or rather, he welcomed death. His heart was broken. He felt the struggle to keep up any longer to be useless. God, the world, humanity—all had abandoned him. It would feel so good to shut eyes forever on the cruel things around him and toward him.

A Visit from Walt Whitman

As luck would have it, at this time I found him. I was passing down Ward No. 6 one day about dusk (4th January, I think), and noticed his glassy eyes, with a look of despair and hopelessness, sunk low in his thin, pallid-brown young face. One learns to divine quickly in the hospital, and as I stopped by him and spoke some commonplace remark (to which he made no reply), I saw as I looked that it was a case for ministering to the affection first and other nourishment and medicines afterward.

I sat down by him without any fuss; talked a little; soon saw that it did him good; led him to talk a little himself; got him somewhat interested; wrote a letter for him to his folks in Massachusetts (to L.H. Campbell, Plymouth County); soothed him down, as I saw he was getting a little too much agitated and tears in his eyes; gave him some small gifts and told him I should come again soon. (He has told me since that this little visit, at that hour, just saved him; a day more and it would have been perhaps too late.)

Of course I did not forget him, for he was a young fellow to interest anyone. He remained very sick—vomiting much every day, frequent diarrhoea, and also something like bronchitis, the doctor said. For a while, I visited him almost every day, cheered him up, took him some little gifts, and gave him small sums of money (he relished a drink of new milk when it was brought through the ward for sale). For a couple of weeks his condition was uncertain; sometimes I thought there was no chance for him at all, but of late he is doing better—is up and dressed and goes around more and more (February 21) every day. He will not die but will recover.

The other evening, passing through the ward, he called me—he wanted to say a few words, particular. I sat down by his side on the cot in the dimness of the long ward, with the wounded soldiers there in their beds, ranging up and down. H. told me I had saved his life. He was in the deepest earnest about it. It was one of those things that repay a soldiers' hospital missionary a thousandfold—one of the hours he never forgets.

A Woman Doctor Treats Casualties from a Black Regiment

Esther Hill Hawks

> Having volunteered for "front-line" duty, Dr. Esther Hawks was shipped south to General Hospital Number 10 for Colored Troops, which was directed by her husband, Dr. J.M. Hawks, and was the first such hospital established by the federal War Department. A keen and sympathetic observer, Dr. Hawks takes a great interest in the attitudes and habits of her charges, which she finds just as engaging as her medical work.
>
> Having carried out the labor of setting up and maintaining an army hospital, the staff of General Hospital Number 10 then witness the worst of what war has to offer, as the wounded soldiers of the Battle of Fort Wagner are carried in.

In Hospital—

The first General Hospital established in Beaufort for colored soldiers, was opened on the 12*th* of Apr. 1863 under the charge of Dr. [J.M.] Hawkes. The first patients admited being the sick and wounded men brought back by Col. Higginson from the Jacksonville expedition! This was another step for colored soldiers as heretofore they had been confined to regimental hospitals which being on a limited scale must necessarily exclude many who need constant care

Excerpted from the July 1863 diary entries of Esther Hill Hawks.

and nursing, besides not having all the appliances for the comfort of the sick, to be found in a large establishment.

Acquaintance with Soap

It was great fun to witness the extreme reluctance, not to say positive disgust with which the patients went through with their initiatory. The first thing to be done when a patient is admitted into hospital is to make him thoroughly acquainted with soap and water, and their pitiful pleadings to be let off from this exercise would have been pathetic if they had'nt been so rediculous. Failing to soften the obdurate hearts of ward-master and Steward, I would be appealed to with all the pathos of negro eloquence. One poor fellow exclaimed with tears in his eyes I know you ai'nt gwine to do it if you can help it—praise de Lord—for I'se done killed foreber if you puts de water all ober me. I neber could stan it in ole massa's time! Surviving the first washing the next was easier tho' they never could be brot' to see the luxury of the thing! The next great difficulty to be overcome, was to get them to sleep between sheets! Poor fellows! they stared aghast on being told to get in between such immaculate whiteness! Of course it *had* to be done, but when those who were able, made their beds, the sheets of some were carefully folded and lain on the outside of the beds, while others spread them out over the blankets, and got into bed, upon the bare mattress—I have found that it takes a great deal of persuasive teaching, with many practical illustrations to enable a *negro soldier* to *make* a *bed.* We were for some time without bed steads—had to wait for them to be made. It took so long to do the smallest job—that I would sometimes almost despair of ever having the house put into decent order for a hospital. The house was one of the Barnwell mansions—and when our troops came here, magnificently furnished but 18 months occupation by soldiers leaves nothing but a filthy shell; Mrs. Strong, wife of our Maj. was appointed nurse by Mrs. Lander, and she and I went about for weeks with a *soaped* rag in hand, overseeing and instructing in the cleaning. We already had between 20 and 30 patients—and this, with getting things in order kept us very busy!

From my first connextion with these people, I have felt quite at home among them, and there is nothing repelant to my feelings about them any more than there is to all dirty people—but here in Hospital we could keep them as clean as we chose, so I circulated among them with the greatest freedom—prescribing for them, ministering to their wants, teaching them, and making myself as thoroughly conversant with their inner lives as I could. I do not think, at this time, without a degree of inhumanity, a hospital for colored, could be conducted on the same rigid principles, as for white troops. These negroes are like ig-

Clara Barton at Fredericksburg

The victory of the Confederate army at the Battle of Bull Run inspired a young Washington clerk, Clara Barton, to volunteer for service as a nurse. Through the next four years, Barton would comfort thousands of sick and dying soldiers, offering medicine, soothing words, or the illusion suffered by many wounded men that she was a distant, loved family member. In A Woman of Valor: Clara Barton and the Civil War, *author Stephen B. Oates relates Barton's nursing in the aftermath of the Battle of Fredericksburg, one of the Union army's bloodiest defeats.*

In the Lacy House, meanwhile, operating surgeons were hard at work in every room, extracting bullets and sawing off limbs, which they threw out the front door. Walt Whitman, who visited the Lacy House while Clara was there, described the hideous sight that greeted him: "at the foot of a tree, immediately in front, a heap of feet, legs, arms, and human fragments, cut, bloody, black and blue, swelled and sickening—in the garden near, a row of graves.". . .

Clara established a soup kitchen on the Lacy House grounds and set to work feeding the broken men inside. They had to step carefully, for the floors were slippery with

norat unformed children, and the difficulty of reasoning them out of an opinion or ideas when it once takes possesion of them, can never be known 'till tried. You talk to willing listeners—they assent heartily to what you say but—they are of the same opinion still.

They are not thoughtful for each others comfort, and I never cease wondering at their indifference to the death of their comrads and even of near friends. There is seldom any display of feelings and in but few instances have I seen sufficient emotion visable to look upon it as grief at the loss of a son or brother. No doubt their religious belief has much to do with this as one of the strongest articles in their creed is, that "no one dies before his time." To return to the Hospital

---

blood. As the surgeons performed amputations, Clara or an assistant was quick to put her pillows under the bloody stumps and offer swills of liquor when the patients awoke, screaming from pain.

The scenes Clara witnessed here would haunt her through all her remaining years. There was the delirious officer, fatally wounded, who confused her for his wife. There were the last of the soldiers retrieved from the field, "half skinned, with frozen arms & legs," who couldn't bear her heat applications until she had administered heavy doses of the surgeon general's liquor. There was Lieutenant Edgar M. Newcomb of the Nineteenth Massachusetts, who lay on a couch hemorrhaging from his wounds, with his stricken brother Charlie at his side. Clara knelt beside him, too, and she and Charlie sang hymns and quoted scripture, and when the dying young man confused Clara for his mother, she "kindly favored the illusion," Charlie remembered, "by shading the light." At last, after hours of agony, Lieutenant Newcomb died. "When I rose from the side of the couch," Clara said later, "I wrung the blood from the bottom of my clothing before I could step, for the weight about my feet."

Stephen B. Oates, *A Woman of Valor: Clara Barton and the Civil War.* New York: The Free Press, 1994.

from which I seldom allow myself to be absent so long, I do not think this, Hospital was admited to the brotherhood of hospitals on quite an even footing. Favors were a little grudingly bestowed. White soldiers near us were hardly respectful to our patients and little annoyances, such as throwing bits of old iron at them, got for the purpose at a blacksmiths'—shop, calling names and other impertenances were of frequent occurance. These troubles came mostly from a Co. of regulars whose camp was quite near, and as the buildings were not very well suited for hospital purposes, it was thought best to change the location, and so run away from many sources of anoyance.

Regimental Surgeon

Dr. H. [Hawks] has been taken from the hospital detailed by Gen. Hunter, to accompany a secret expedition to the coast of Florida. Meanwhile no Surgeon being sent to take charge, of the hospital, I am left manager of not only the affairs of the Hospital, but have to attend Surgeons' call for the 2nd [S.C. Volunteers] and without a Surgeon—so every morning at 9 o'clock the disabled are marched down to the hospital in charge of a Sergent and I hold surgeons call, for hospital and Regt. and with great success; on the back piazza sending some to duty and taking into the hospital such as need extra care. An occasional chronic 'shirk' will complain to the Col. that, "dat woman ca'nt do me no gud, she ca'nt see my pain" but he gets no sympathy from the Col. and is obliged to go on duty if I so mark him. So for three weeks I performed the duties of hospital and Regimental Surg. doing the work so well that the neglect to supply a regular officers was not discovered at Hd. Qrtrs. I suppose I could not have done this if my brother had not been hospital steward—or if the patients had been white men—but these negroes are so like children that I feel no hesitancy in serving them!

The last of May Dr. Greenleaf assumed charge, and I returned to my teaching, (having had the experience of two months hospital life), with many feelings of regret expressed by the patients and felt by my self. As the patients were removed to another building I continued to occupy the same house, and as the Fates ordained, I went into the old school where I first commenced teaching on my arrival here. The school was large and I exhausted so five weeks trial closed it by prostrating me with fever, and in two weeks more the schools were all closed by, most of the buildings being wanted for hospital uses and the teachers such as did not run home on the first alarm, as nurses.

Battle Wounds

July 18*th*! never to be forgotten day! After many days of anxious waiting the news came, "Prepare immediately to receive 500 wounded men," indeed they were already at the dock! and before morning we had taken possession of the building where our first hospital was started. I had been carried, a few days previous to Dr. Durrants to stay with Mrs. D. during the absence of her husband in Bermuda so the house was soon cleared. 150 of the brave boys from the 54*th* Mass. Col. Shaw's Regt. were brought to us and laid on blankets on the floor all mangled and ghastly. What a terrible sight it was! It was 36 hours since the awful struggle at Ft. Wagna [Wagner] and nothing had been done for them. We had no beds, and no means even of building a fire, but the colored people came promptly to our aid and almost before we knew what we needed they brought us buckets full of nice broth and gruels, pitchers of lemonade, fruits, cakes, vegetables indeed everything needed for the immediate wants of the men was furnished—not for one day but for many (Then too the Sanitary Com. [Commission] blessed us with its ready aid. Everything for our immediate wants was furnished and in 24 hours the poor fellows were lying with clean clothes and dressed wounds in comfortable beds, and we breathed freely again) before setting about creating a hospital: no one, unless they have had the experience can, imagine the amount of work and worry needed in setting one of these vast military machines in motion! and in this case humanity demanded that the poor fellows who had fought so bravely, should be first attended to. The colored

people still continued to supply delicacies and more substantial aid came from the citizens and Sanitary Com. (It
was a busy time, and the amount of work done in that 24
hours, by the two surgeons, and one sick woman is tiresome
to remember! The only thing that sustained us was the patient endurance of those stricken heroes lying before us,
with their ghastly wounds cheerful & courageous, many a
poor fellow sighing that his right arm was shattered beyond
hope of striking another blow for freedom! Only a few
weeks before we had welcomed them as they marched so
proudly through our streets with their idolized leader Col.
Shaw, at their head!—How all the colored people cheered
and gloried in their fine appearance—and now the people
are so eager to show their pride in them that they constantly deny themselves in order to bring gifts to the hospital!)—

Several severe cases of gangreen poisn'd the air and had
to be removed outside—out breathing the tainted atmosphere and overwork caused me a relaps and disheartened, I
prepared to be sent North—but God had more work for me
here and after a week of pain I returned to my post and the
hearty "God bless you we are glad to see you back with us"
compensated for much weariness.

"I'm Not Afraid to Die"

. . . Three brothers, noble, stalwart men, lay side by side severely wounded! The fourth who had left home with them
fell and was buried with his Col. at Ft. Wagna [Wagner]!
They had left home, giving up useful and lucrative employ-
ment, with no idle thoughts of pleasure, nor yet from mere
recklessness, but with an earnest, hopeful purpose in their
hearts that they too, might help win for themselves and their
race a *country* God forgive the Nation's weak and wicked
policy which withholds from such its fullest protection!—
"We offered to go when the war broke out," they told me,
"but no one would have us, and as soon as Gov. Andrew
gave us a chance all the boys in our place were ready, hardly one who could carry a musket stayed at home." An elder
brother of theirs, who had a family to provide for, remained

at home: but when the 55*th* [Mass. Vol. Inf.] came out he was with them (Their name is Crunkleton [Krunkleton]). Another, a young man from Cincinnatti, educated at Oberlin, of ability and good mental capacity—An orderly Sergt. in Co. A has a promise of promotion for his brave and gallant conduct at Ft Wagna [Wagner]—has the real worth and material for a good officer, but he is a very trying patient, chafes and frets because he cannot be with his Company— he is not so patient and uncomplaining as the others—is more ambitious. He is very neat about his person and any disorder about his bed or the room frets him.

O, Mrs. Hawks, he exclaimed one day, when I had been talking to him of that higher courage which enables us to bear the defeat of cherished hopes and ambitions, "It isn't that I can't die if necessary; I'm not afraid to die, I came to die fighting for the rights of the black man What I want is to go back to my regiment and go with them wherever they are called to go, but I cant stay here, inactive, and not know what has become of my Col. or my Co [Company]! I know the Dr. tells me I cannot do anything for months. I wish he exclaimed passionately, the ball of that miserable traitor had ended my life rather than made me a miserable cripple! and the strong man wept such bitter tears as I hope never to see again. My heart went out to the noble fellow and I comforted him as best I could thanking God for the rare boon of ministering to such spirits My brave Sergt. is not greatly beloved by those under him, he is arbitrary and a little tyranical but a good disciplinarian. He received the injury to his spine after being wounded and thrown from the paraphet by a cannon ball passing so close to him as to carry away his cartridge box and shiver his musket. In writing to his friends he asked me not to say he was injured in the back. "They would'nt understand he said, and I cant bear to have them think for a moment that Sergt. Morgan's back was to the rebels!"

One young man, Jonny Lott, one of my especial pets a handsome boy, a mere boy, who had come from the far west to bear his part of suffering, had his right arm shattered and his life was, for many days, despaired of, and in the long days of weary restlessness I learned the brave spirit of the boy well. He was well educated—had taught a term in a colored school. One day I had been reading beside his bed I said to him, Johny do you ever wish that you had been born white? He kept quiet a few moments, his eyes covered with their long silken fringes, then with a quick nervous movement, looking up with a dewy moisture in his great beautiful eyes, he said "I always felt glad to be just what I am, a black boy with no drop of white blood in me There is a chance now to do a great deal if one has the heart for it and I am ready to give my other arm, or my life if necessary, for my race!" Was'nt that a noble answer for a boy of seventeen black or white. How proud I was of him! God grant that his days may be long and full of usefulness!

Chapter 7

Appomattox and Victory

Chapter Preface

The election of 1864 returned Abraham Lincoln to office, with the promise that the war would be carried on to the bitter end. Although the North had won important victories, many Northerners considered the conflict a stalemate and believed that the South would never be completely defeated. A large faction of war-weary Northerners, among them Horace Greeley, the influential editor of the *New York Tribune,* demanded a cease-fire and negotiations to end the war. But Lincoln would accept nothing less than the complete restoration of the Union, and President Jefferson Davis of the Confederacy would accept no terms for peace except the total independence of the South.

In the spring of 1865, the outcome of the war was finally decided on the battlefield. After a long campaign through eastern Virginia, the Confederate army, commanded by Robert E. Lee, was in a desperate situation. In April, troops under Grant's command seized the railroads supplying Richmond, forcing Lee to abandon the Confederate capital. When Grant and General Philip H. Sheridan cut off Lee's escape to the west, Lee asked for terms of surrender. The agreement ending hostilities between Lee's and Grant's armies officially ending the war was signed at Appomattox Courthouse, Virginia.

The enlisted men and officers of the Union armies, their terms of service ended, returned to their homes and their farms by the thousands. Northern industry began a difficult adjustment to a peacetime economy, while officials of the federal government debated, sometimes bitterly, the terms for readmittance of the Confederate states into the Union.

While the economic adjustments and political battles that followed the war proceeded, the freed slaves of the South had to make the greatest transformation of all—from slaves to free citizens. The process was made all the harder because whites resisted the idea of equality for blacks. In many places, the "freedmen" were still prevented from voting, despite ratification in 1870 of the Fifteenth Amendment, which guaranteed the right of all citizens, black or white, to vote. The Thirteenth Amendment, ratified in 1865, had abolished slavery, but in many places, blacks could not own land or pursue certain occupations; they could not move freely about the streets, appear as witnesses in court, or attend the same schools as white students.

To assist the freedmen, Congress had created the Freedmen's Bureau in March, 1865. The Freedmen's Bureau issued emergency rations (to black and white southerners), built new hospitals, established courts to decide labor disputes, and founded schools for African American students. The Bureau also assisted white refugees who were homeless and now faced starvation. The Bureau served the aims of the former Northern abolitionists who, their goal of emancipation having been achieved, now hoped to overcome the bitter legacy of slavery and a devastating four-year war.

Witness at Appomattox

Horace Porter

In the first week of April 1865, with his generals outmaneuvered and his troops starving and demoralized, General
Robert E. Lee asked General Ulysses S. Grant for the Union's
terms for surrender. Grant returned the message and arranged
for a meeting with Lee at the village of Appomattox Courthouse in southern Virginia.

It was the first time Lee and Grant had met since the Mexican War of the late 1840s. At that time, both men were fighting for the government of the United States. Now they met as
adversaries, with Grant having won the victory for the Union
and Lee losing as the commander of the Confederate armies.
Knowing the historical importance of their meeting, and that
the North and the South must follow their lead and begin to
heal the terrible wounds of the war, both men acted with dignity and reserve, determined to bring the war to an end on the
most conciliatory terms possible. General Horace Porter, one
of Grant's staff officers, witnessed the proceedings and gave
the following account in his Civil War memoirs.

L ee now mounted his horse, and directed Colonel Marshall to accompany him. They started for Appomattox
Court-house in company with Babcock, followed by a
mounted orderly. When the party reached the village they
met one of its residents, named Wilmer McLean, who was
told that General Lee wished to occupy a convenient room
in some house in the town. McLean ushered them into the

Excerpted from Horace Porter, *Campaigning with Grant* (New York: Century, 1897).

sitting-room of one of the first houses he came to; but upon looking about, and seeing that it was small and unfurnished, Lee proposed finding something more commodious and better fitted for the occasion. McLean then conducted the party to his own house, about the best one in the town, where they awaited General Grant's arrival.

The house had a comfortable wooden porch with seven steps leading up to it. A hall ran through the middle from front to back, and upon each side was a room having two windows, one in front and one in rear. Each room had two doors opening into the hall. The building stood a little distance back from the street, with a yard in front, and to the left on entering was a gate for carriages, and a roadway running to a stable in rear. We entered the grounds by this gate, and dismounted. In the yard were seen a fine, large gray horse which proved to be General Lee's favorite animal, called "Traveler," and a good-looking, dark-colored mare belonging to Colonel Marshall. An orderly in gray was in charge of them, and had taken off their bridles to let them crop the grass.

General Grant mounted the steps and entered the house. As he stepped into the hall, Colonel Babcock, who had seen his approach from the window, opened the door of the room on the left, in which he had been sitting with General Lee and Colonel Marshall awaiting General Grant's arrival. The general passed in, and as Lee arose and stepped forward, Grant extended his hand, saying, "General Lee," and the two shook hands cordially. The members of the staff, Generals Sheridan and Ord, and some other general officers who had gathered in the front yard, remained outside, feeling that General Grant would probably prefer his first interview with General Lee to be, in a measure, private. In a few minutes Colonel Babcock came to the front door, and, making a motion with his hat toward the sitting-room, said: "The general says come in." It was then about half-past one on Sunday, the 9th of April. . . .

The Two Commanders

The contrast between the two commanders was singularly striking, and could not fail to attract marked attention as they sat, six or eight feet apart, facing each other. General Grant, then nearly forty-three years of age, was five feet eight inches in height, with shoulders slightly stooped. His hair and full beard were nut-brown, without a trace of gray in them. He had on his single-breasted blouse of dark-blue flannel, unbuttoned in front and showing a waistcoat underneath. He wore an ordinary pair of top-boots, with his trousers inside, and was without spurs. The boots and portions of his clothes were spattered with mud. He had worn a pair of thread gloves of a dark-yellow color, which had had taken off on entering the room. His felt "sugar-loaf," stiff-brimmed hat was resting on his lap. He had no sword or sash, and a pair of shoulder-straps was all there was about

The Civil War Ends Quietly at Appomattox

In his epic series of Civil War histories, Bruce Catton chronicled the war's battles great and small, military strategy, the uncommon bravery of ordinary soldiers, incidents of civilian life and the story behind the decisions and machinations of political leaders on both sides. In A Stillness at Appomattox, *Catton ends his series with a description of the sudden calm that reigned in the neighborhood of Appomattox, Virginia, on the surrender of General Lee to General Grant.*

All up and down the lines the men blinked at one another, unable to realize that the hour they had waited for so long was actually at hand. There was a truce, they could see that, and presently the word was passed that Grant and Lee were going to meet in the little village that lay now between the two lines, and no one could doubt that Lee was going to surrender. It was Palm Sunday, and they would all live to see Easter, and with the guns quieted it might be easier to comprehend the mystery and promise of that day. Yet the fact of peace and no more killing and an open road home seems to have been too big to grasp, right at the moment, and in the enormous silence that lay upon the field men rehim to designate his rank. In fact, aside from these, his uniform was that of a private soldier.

Lee, on the other hand, was six feet and one inch in height and erect for one of his age for he was Grant's senior by sixteen years. His hair and full beard were a silver-gray, and thick, except that the hair had become a little thin in front. He wore a new uniform of Confederate gray, buttoned to the throat, and a handsome sword and sash. The sword was of exceedingly fine workmanship, and the hilt was studded with jewels. It had been presented to him by some ladies in England who sympathized with the cause he represented. His top-boots were comparatively new, and had on them near the top some ornamental stitching of red silk. Like his

---

membered that they had marched far and were very tired, and they wondered when the wagon trains would come up with rations. . . .

A Pennsylvanian in the V Corps dodged past the skirmish line and strolled into the lines of the nearest Confederate regiment, and half a century after the war he recalled it with a glow: ". . . as soon as got among these boys I felt and was treated as well as if I had been among our own boys, and a person would of thought we were of the same army and had been Fighting under the Same Flag."

Down by the roadside near Appomattox Court House, Sheridan and Ord and other officers sat and waited while a brown-bearded little man in a mud-spattered uniform rode up. They all saluted him, and there was a quiet interchange of greetings, and then General Grant tilted his head toward the village and asked: "Is General Lee up here?"

Sheridan replied that he was, and Grant said: "Very well. Let's go up."

The little cavalcade went trotting along the road to the village, and all around them the two armies waited in silence. As the generals neared the end of their ride, a Yankee band in a field near the town struck up "Auld Lang Syne."

Bruce Catton, *A Stillness at Appomattox.* New York: Anchor Books, 1990.

uniform, they were clean. On the boots were handsome spurs with large rowels. A felt hat which in color matched pretty closely that of his uniform, and a pair of long, gray buckskin gauntlets, lay beside him on the table. We endeavored afterward to learn how it was that he wore such fine clothes, and looked so much as if he had turned out to go to church that Sunday afternoon, while with us our outward garb scarcely rose to the dignity even of the "shabby-genteel." One explanation was that when his headquarters wagons had been pressed so closely by our cavalry a few days before, it was found that his officers would have to destroy all their baggage, except the clothes they carried on their backs; and each one naturally selected the newest suit he had, and sought to propitiate the god of destruction by a sacrifice of his second-best. Another reason given was that, in deference to General Grant, General Lee had dressed himself with special care for the purpose of the meeting.

Small Talk

Grant began the conversation by saying: "I met you once before, General Lee, while we were serving in Mexico, when you came over from General Scott's headquarters to visit Garland's brigade, to which I then belonged. I have always remembered your appearance, and I think I should have recognized you anywhere." "Yes," replied General Lee; "I know I met you on that occasion, and I have often thought of it, and tried to recollect how you looked, but I have never been able to recall a single feature." After some further mention of Mexico, General Lee said: "I suppose, General Grant, that the object of our present meeting is fully understood. I asked to see you to ascertain upon what terms you would receive the surrender of my army." General Grant replied: "The terms I propose are those stated substantially in my letter of yesterday; that is, the officers and men surrendered to be paroled and disqualified from taking up arms again until properly exchanged, and all arms, ammunition, and supplies to be delivered up as captured property." Lee nodded an assent, and said: "Those are about the conditions which I expected would be proposed." General Grant then continued: "Yes; I think our correspondence indicated pretty clearly the action that would be taken at our meeting, and I hope it may lead to a general suspension of hostilities, and be the means of preventing any further loss of life."

Lee inclined his head as indicating his accord with this wish, and General Grant then went on to talk some length in a very pleasant vein about the prospects of peace. Lee was evidently anxious to proceed to the formal work of the surrender, and he brought the subject up again by saying:

"I presume, General Grant, we have both carefully considered the proper steps to be taken, and I would suggest that you commit to writing the terms you have proposed, so that they may be formally acted upon."

"Very well," replied Grant; "I will write them out." And calling for his manifold order-book, he opened it, laid it on a small oval wooden table which Colonel Parker brought to him from the rear of the room, and proceeded to write the terms. The leaves [pages] had been so prepared that three impressions of the writing were made. He wrote very rapidly, and did not pause until he had finished the sentence ending with "officers appointed by me to receive them." Then he looked toward Lee, and his eyes seemed to be resting on the handsome sword that hung at that officer's side. He said afterward that this set him to thinking that it would be an unnecessary humiliation to require the officers to surrender their swords, and a great hardship to deprive them of their personal baggage and horses; and after a short pause he wrote the sentence: "This will not embrace the side-arms of the officers, nor their private horses or baggage."

When he had finished the letter he called Colonel Parker to his side, and looked it over with him, and directed him as they went along to interline [add] six or seven words, and to strike out the word "their," which had been repeated. When this had been done the general took the manifold writer [copy-book] in his right hand, extended his arm toward Lee, and started to rise from his chair to hand the book to him. As I was standing equally distant from them, with my back to the front window, I stepped forward, took the book, and passed it to General Lee. The terms were as follows:

> Appomattox Court-house, Va., April 9, 1865.
> General R.E. Lee, Commanding C.S.A.
>
> General: In accordance with the substance of my letter to you of the 8th inst., I propose to receive the surrender of the Army of Northern Virginia on the following terms, to wit: Rolls of all the officers and men to be made in duplicate, one copy to be given to an officer to be designated by me, the other to be retained by such officer or officers as you may designate. The officers to give their individual paroles [promises] not to take up arms against the Government of the United States until properly [exchanged], and each company or regimental commander to sign a like parole for the men of their commands. The arms, artillery, and public property to be parked and stacked and turned over to the officers appointed by me to receive them. This will not embrace the side-arms of the officers, nor their private horses or baggage. This done, each officer and man will be allowed to return to his home, not to be disturbed by the United States authorities so long as they observe their paroles and the laws in force where they may reside.
>
> > Very respectfully,
> > U.S. Grant,
> > Lieutenant-general.

Lee pushed aside some books and two brass candlesticks which were on the table, then took the book and laid it down before him, while he drew from his pocket a pair of steel-rimmed spectacles, and wiped the glasses carefully with his handkerchief. He crossed his legs, adjusted the spectacles very slowly and deliberately, took up the draft of the terms, and proceeded to read them attentively. They consisted of two pages. When be reached the top line of the second page, he looked up, and said to General Grant: "After the words 'until properly' the word 'exchanged' seems to be omitted. You doubtless intended to use that word."

"Why, yes," said Grant; "I thought I had put in the word 'exchanged.'"

"I presumed it had been omitted inadvertently," continued Lee; "and, with your permission, I will mark where it should be inserted."

"Certainly," Grant replied.

Private Horses

Lee felt in his pocket as if searching for a pencil, but he did not seem to be able to find one. Seeing this, I handed him my lead-pencil. During the rest of the interview he kept twirling this pencil in his fingers and occasionally tapping the top of the table with it. When he handed it back, it was carefully treasured by me as a memento of the occasion. When Lee came to the sentence about the officers' side-arms, private horses and baggage, he showed for the first time during the reading of the letter a slight change of countenance, and was evidently touched by this act of generosity. It was doubtless the condition mentioned to which he particularly alluded when he looked toward General Grant, as he finished reading, and said with some degree of warmth in his manner, "This will have a very happy effect upon my army."

General Grant then said: "Unless you have some suggestions to make in regard to the form in which I have stated the terms, I will have a copy of the letter made in ink, and sign it."

"There is one thing I should like to mention," Lee replied, after a short pause. "The cavalrymen and artillerists own their own horses in our army. Its organization in this respect differs from that of the United States." This expression attracted the notice of our officers present, as showing how firmly the conviction was grounded in his mind that we were two distinct countries. He continued: "I should like to understand whether these men will be permitted to retain their horses."

"You will find that the terms as written do not allow this," General Grant replied; "only the officers are permitted to take their private property."

Lee read over the second page of the letter again, and then said: "No, I see the terms do not allow it; that is clear." His face showed plainly that he was quite anxious to have this concession made; and Grant said very promptly, and without giving Lee time to make a direct request:

"Well, the subject is quite new to me. Of course I did not know that any private soldiers owned their animals; but I think we have fought the last battle of the war,—I sincerely hope so,—and that the surrender of this army will be followed soon by that of all the others; and I take it that most of the men in the ranks are small farmers, and as the country has been so raided by the two armies, it is doubtful whether they will be able to put in a crop to carry themselves and their families through the next winter without the aid of the horses they are now riding, and I will arrange it in this way: I will not change the terms as now written, but I will instruct the officers I shall appoint to receive the paroles to let all the men who claim to own a horse or mule take the animals home with them to work their little farms." (This expression has been quoted in various forms, and has been the subject of some dispute. I give the exact words used.)

The Surrender

Lee now looked greatly relieved, and though anything but a demonstrative man, he gave every evidence of his appreciation of this concession, and said: "This will have the best possible effect upon the men. It will be very gratifying, and will do much toward conciliating our people." He handed the draft of the terms back to General Grant, who called Colonel T.S. Bowers of the staff to him, and directed him to make a copy in ink. Bowers was a little nervous, and he turned the matter over to Colonel Parker, whose handwriting presented a better appearance than that of any one else on the staff. Parker sat down to write at the oval table, which he had moved again to the rear of the room. Wilmer McLean's domestic resources in the way of ink now became the subject of a searching investigation, but it was found that the contents of the conical-shaped stoneware inkstand with a paper stopper which he produced appeared to be participating in the general breaking up, and had disappeared. Colonel Marshall now came to the rescue, and took from his pocket a small boxwood inkstand, which was put at Parker's service, so that, after all, we had to fall back upon the resources of the enemy to furnish the "stage properties" for the final scene in the memorable military drama.

Colonel Marshall then took a seat on the sofa beside Sheridan and Ingalls. When the terms had been copied, Lee directed his military secretary to draw up for his signature a letter of acceptance. Colonel Marshall wrote out a draft of such a letter, making it formal, beginning with, "I have the honor to acknowledge," etc. General Lee took it, and after reading it over very carefully, directed that these formal expressions be stricken out, and that the letter be otherwise shortened. He afterward went over it again, and seemed to change some words, and then told the colonel to make a final copy in ink. When it came to providing the paper, it was found that we had the only supply of that important ingredient in the recipe for surrendering an army, so we gave a few pages to the colonel. The letter when completed read as follows:

Headquarters, Army of Northern Virginia,
April 9,1865.
General: I have received your letter of this date containing the terms of the surrender of the Army of Northern Virginia as proposed by you. As they are substantially the same as those expressed in your letter of the 8th inst., they are accepted. I will proceed to designate the proper officers to carry the stipulations into effect.
Very respectfully, your obedient servant,
R.E. Lee,
General.

Lieutenant-general U.S. Grant
Commanding Armies of U.S.

"Death to All Traitors"

Joseph Rutherford

Lee's surrender at Appomattox brought joy and relief to thousands of Northern soldiers and their families at home. It also released pent-up feelings of anger and national betrayal on the part of those who had risked their lives fighting for the cause of the Union.

From Alexandria, Virginia, Surgeon Joseph Rutherford of the 17th Vermont Infantry wrote the following letter to his wife Hannah on April 29, 1865, less than three weeks after the surrender. In the letter, Rutherford tries to ease the anxiety of his wife, who fears reprisals from the people surrounding him in enemy territory in Virginia. For his part, Rutherford shows a zealous devotion to the war his side has just won and a determination to see the Confederacy and its "hell born traitors" punished for their disloyalty.

Alexandria Va Apr 29th 1865
My dear Wife,

I have just received your letter of the 24th and hasten to reply to it.

I do not wonder at your anxiety in fact I some expected just such a letter from you for my long silence. that is long for me. If you had been in my place for the last 10 days you would not think strange of my seeming neglect. We have marched over 300 miles besides going a long way by water and our mail facilities have been very limited and I did not

Joseph C. Rutherford, letter to Hannah Rutherford, April 29, 1865.

feel very much like writing if I had the convenien[ce]s for doing so. Then again I had nothing particularly interesting to write. You should know by this time that if any thing was wrong with me you would be informed of it at once. Though I have not (the wind blows my paper all about) written—you may rest assured that you nor our dear children are never out of mind. I dont think I am much sorry that I did let a few days slip by without writing as you will better appreciate my poor letters. You seem to feel very anxious about my exposing myself to traitors etc Now I can well appreciate your anxiety but as I *never* visit any of the houses of the inhabitants there can be very little danger to myself. then what good could an injury to me do the cussed traitors?

You ask my opinion of the affairs of the nation. What can *I* say—any more than I have often said—that we are coming out all right. The thing no doubt looks dark to you who are so far from the strife and field of battle, but to us every thing is looked upon as the fulfillment of the nations destiny. God rules our nation and the events of our terrible war. let us bow in submision to his will, and act the part set for us to the best of our abilities.

If Sherman has done as it is said he did—Why I think he has *dulled*—in other words made a great blunder— But so much have I become to believe in the ultimate designs of the great Ruler of all things that I feel it was intended that greater good might accrue to the nation from it. It opens the eyes of the people to the gross folly of being too lenient to these hell born traitors not only at the South but in the midst of our N.E. [New England] homes. We are all coming home soon: and our first work will be to clean out every traitor and tory [opponent of the Republican party]—that act as foul ulcers in the living flesh of our homes. We soldiers have *vowed* it upon the alter of our country and you may depend the poisonous blood of these treacherous villians will flow freely, for the lives of many of our noble soldiers they have been the means of sacrificing. God have mercy on them for we wont—*No! Never.*

I am more surprised that Friend Seargent did not take the

life of that rotten hearted scoundrel than I should have been if he had—Robinson might as well learn now as ever that his life will not be worth the asking if he is found in the country when our troops return home.* You may think me excited and so I am but it is an excitement that nothing but the just punishment of traitors will allay. The country will never be safe while they are allowed to walk its surface or breath the air of heaven—Death to all traitors is our watch word—

I am surprised that Lt Seargent should make such a mistake [having] been in the service as long as he has. Ask him if a Surgeon dont wear the *Gold leaf?* made thus

A Surgeon ranks as Major. A Captains badge is the two bars—the Strap made thus

A surgeon ranks as major of Cavalry which gives him more pay than major of Infantry. I am glad to learn that our friend Page is improving—dont forget to remember me to him and his excelent Wife. I have got to writing I hardly know when to stop—but the wind flirts my paper about so much that it is next to impossible to write. I have plenty of elbow room for I am under the broad canopy of heaven where the gentle zephers have their full play.

I think you will see us all home about the 1st of June. Remember me to our dear children and accept the undying love of your

Affectionate husband
J.C. Rutherford

* The identity of "Robinson" and the exact nature of his transgression are unknown.

Captain Adams Musters Out

John G.B. Adams

Captain John G.B. Adams, of the 19th Massachusetts Volunteers, survived the harrowing experience of capture and imprisonment by the enemy. While being held at the notorious prison facility at Camp Sorghum, near Columbia, South Carolina, Adams escaped and was recaptured. In the final months of the war, Adams was put on a train along with hundreds of other bedraggled and hungry Union prisoners, bound for Charlotte, North Carolina. Knowing that the Confederacy was in its death throes, the prisoners desperately hoped for an exchange, which would allow them to return home as long as they signed a parole—a promise not to bear arms until a formal exchange was signed. Finally, on March 1, 1865, Captain Adams, along with 200 other Union prisoners, was brought to Rocky Point, North Carolina, and released to the Union lines.

Relieved to have survived the prison camps and the war, and unable to take up arms again, Captain Adams returned to his Massachusetts home. For the officers and enlisted men of the Union army, life began to return to normal in the late spring and summer of 1865. Invited to take part in a July 4 parade of his regiment in Boston, Captain Adams finds that nearly all of the regiment's members have better things to do.

One afternoon at three o'clock the order was given to "fall in." It was an uncommon call at this hour, and [prisoner] "exchange" thoughts came to all. Soon the adju-

Excerpted from John G.B. Adams, *Reminiscences of the Nineteenth Massachusetts Regiment* (Boston: Wright, Potter, 1899).

tant introduced us to a new commander, a Dutchman who had just come from the north, having been captured at Gettysburg. Said he: "Ghentlemens, I comes to take command of you. I have been in Fort Delaware fifteen months. You peoples teach me how to behave myself. I does for you all I can. You treats me like ghentleman, I treats you like ghentlemen. This place not fit for hogs. I sends in one hundred load of straw, right away, quick. Break ranks, march!" He went through our quarters and swore worse than we could at our treatment. He then went to the hospital, had a row with the surgeon because he had done nothing to make us comfortable, and kicked up a row generally in our behalf. We felt that "the morning light was breaking" for us, and that we should now be made comfortable. The major came in the next day with more suggestions, but in a day or two we saw him no more. He was not the man the rebels wanted, as they were not anxious for our comfort, and his official head was removed as soon as he made requisition for the straw.

Prisoner Exchange

On [February] 20th, two hundred of us left to be exchanged. We had quite a pleasant ride to Salisbury [North Carolina]. Here I saw some of my men, the first I had seen since we left them at Macon, in July. I remember two, my first sergeant, James Smith, and Private Jerry Kelly. I dare not undertake to describe their condition; they were nearly starved to death and could only walk by the aid of sticks. They told me of the other boys captured,—that Lubin, a young recruit, had died three days after entering Andersonville [a notorious prisoner-of-war camp in Georgia]; that Sergt. Geo. E. Morse and Levi Wooffindale of Company G, and many others, had died at Andersonville, Florence and other prisons; for, like us, they had been carted from one place to another, but their faces brightened as they said, "Not one of the boys went back on the old flag." I had been proud of the 19th regiment from the first day I joined it, but never did I see the time when I loved and respected those boys more than that day.

More than thirty thousand were crowded into the pen at Andersonville. They had seen their comrades die at the rate of two hundred a day; they had been offered plenty of food and clothing, and no fighting, if they would renounce their allegiance to the old flag and join the southern Confederacy, but they said, "*No! No! Death before dishonor!*" and waited to join their comrades beneath the starry flag if they lived to be free, if not to join those who had been loyal and true in the camp on the other shore.

We went from Charlotte to Goldsboro, where we arrived the next morning. Here we saw the worst sight that the eyes of mortal ever gazed upon. Two long trains of platform cars, loaded with our men, came in. They had been three days on the road, expecting to be exchanged at Wilmington, but as the city was being bombarded, were turned back. As they were unloaded not one in fifty was able to stand. Many were left dead on the cars, the guards rolling them off as they would logs of wood; most of them were nearly naked, and their feet and hands were frozen; they had lost their reason; could not tell the State they came from, their regiment or company. We threw them what rations we had, and they would fight for them like dogs, rolling over each other in their eagerness to get the least morsel. I remember one poor fellow who had lost his teeth by scurvy; he would pick raw corn out of the dirt by the railroad track and try to eat it. We gave them everything we had. I took my only shirt from my back and threw it to them; others did the same. The rebels allowed us to mingle with them, and with tears streaming down our cheeks we did what we could.

Lieutenant McGinnis and I were looking for our men, when we found one named Thompson, of his company. He was a noble fellow, one of the largest men in the regiment; the only clothing he had on was part of a shirt and that was covered with vermin; he had lost his sight and was almost gone; he died while we were with him. I took a little fellow in my arms and carried him across the street; he could not have been over sixteen years old, and did not weigh more than fifty pounds; he died just as I laid him down.

The men were marched to a camp, and the route was strewn with dead and dying. The citizens gathered round, but I saw or heard no expression of sympathy. One of our officers said, "My time is out, but all I ask is a chance to once more take the field; I would try and get square." A rebel officer heard him, and replied, "You are just the man I would like to meet." Our officer stepped out and said, "Here I am, I have been more than a year in prison, but I will whip you or any other rebel you can furnish." The rebel sneaked away, and said he would not disgrace himself by fighting a Yankee except in battle. We wished he had given our man a chance.

We were again ordered on board the cars, and it was reported that we were going to Richmond for exchange. We went as far as Raleigh, where we halted, left the train and marched to an old camp. There were a few houses standing, but not enough to hold one-fourth of our number. The rain came down in torrents and we stood all night under the trees. I never passed a more uncomfortable night, for besides being wet and cold, I suffered with hunger.

Parole

On the 23d they loaded us on the cars again, and had just started, when the engine ran off the track. This time the cause was an open switch. We believed that the switch was intentionally left open, but the train ran so slowly that we were off the cars as soon as the engine left the track, and no one was hurt. We were then taken to Camp Holmes, some three miles out of the city, and paroles [promises made by captured soldiers not to bear arms or fight again] were made out and signed. This settled the question of escape and we began to feel happy. We remained here until the 26th, and began to think that the parole was another trap to keep us with a small guard. All were excited, and had they not moved three hundred at noon I don't believe a man able to travel would have remained in camp that night.

On the morning of the 27th we found ourselves in Goldsboro again, and were marched to camp. Here we had to sign another parole, as the first was not made out properly. All these delays were terrible; our nervous condition was such that we could not sleep, and days were as long as weeks. We received very little food, and here I sold the last thing that would bring a dollar, the buttons on my jacket. These brought me eighteen dollars,—two dollars each. It would buy just food enough to sustain life. At night the rebels gave us some rations, but, hungry as we were, we sent all to the enlisted men.

Free at Last!

The 28th, at five P.M., we again went on board the train, and at daylight, March 1, were at Rocky Point, three miles from our lines. Here we left the cars, the rebel guard formed in line and we were counted through. As soon as we passed the rebel lines we ran down the road, cheering and singing. About a quarter of a mile further on the guard stopped us and formed us in some kind of order. Although we were with the boys in blue we did not fully realize that we were free, and clung to all our prison outfit. We marched about a mile to the northeast bridge, on the Cape Fear River, and on the other side saw an arch covered with the stars and stripes. In the centre of the arch, surrounded by a wreath of evergreen, were the words, "Welcome, Brothers!" I have no idea what the joy will be when I pass through the pearly gates and march up the golden streets of the New Jerusalem, but if it is half as great as it was the morning of March 1, 1865, when for the first time for nearly nine months I saw the old flag, I shall be satisfied.

One who did not understand the situation would have thought that an insane asylum had been turned loose. We hugged each other, laughed, cried, prayed, rolled over in the dirt, and expressed our joy, each in his own way. Those who had clung to their meal threw it high in air, and for once meal was plenty.

The 6th Connecticut were encamped near, and their band played national airs as we marched over the bridge. We also found our true friend, the colored man, not as a slave, but as a man and a comrade, clothed in loyal blue and fighting for a flag that never, until President Lincoln signed the Emancipation Proclamation, had protected him. As soon as we were over the bridge they began to provide for our wants. Hard-tack boxes were burst open, coffee and meat were furnished in abundance; but we had been starving so long that we did not think it would last, and I remember that I packed my old jacket—now fastened together with wooden pins—full, and as it settled down crowded in more. We drank so much coffee that we were nearly intoxicated.

We cheered the boys who had provided so well for us, and started for Wilmington. We did not march, but hobbled along as best we could, anxious to get as far as possible from the rebels. We clung to our instruments, and carried the big base viol by turns. It was my turn to carry it, and McGinnis and I started down the railroad. We had gone but a short distance when we met an officer, who asked me where I got the big fiddle. I toll him I had played it in church before I enlisted; that I carried it with me when I left home and had it on picket; was in the middle of a tune when the rebels came on me, and as I could not stop playing was captured. The man looked at me and said, "I believe that's a d—d lie." "Well," I said, "you have a right to think so," and we moved along. I do not remember what became of the instrument.

From Dirty Prisoner to Respectable Free Man

Arriving at Wilmington, we were collected together and rations were served. Here we were placed under guard to prevent our eating too much, but we would capture the rations each side of us and fill our pockets. As soon as we had eaten all we could, we would pass out, and in half an hour try to flank in again. The sanitary commission were on hand with barrels of weak milk punch and gave us all we wanted; as we wanted everything to eat or drink that we saw we destroyed large quantities of it. While standing on the street an officer rode up whom I recognized as Col. Henry A. Hale, formerly a captain in my regiment. He was serving on the staff of the general commanding the department. He took me to a gunboat in the river and bought me a suit of sailor's clothes. After a good bath I was transformed from a dirty prisoner into a respectable Jack Tar. I threw my old clothes overboard, and they floated down the stream freighted with a crew which had clung to me closer than a brother for the past nine months, and whose united voices I thought I heard singing "A life on the ocean wave" as they passed out to sea.

I returned to the city and walked about, often meeting some of the men of my regiment, among them Michael O'Leary of Company F, who looked as though he had just come off dress parade, having a new uniform and his shoes nicely polished. He was delighted to see me, said that the rebels had urged him to take the oath of allegiance, but he had told them he could never look Mary Ann in the face if he went back on the old flag. He told me of a number of the men who had died, among them my old friend Mike Scannell. That night I stood in front of the theatre, my hands in my empty pockets, wondering if I should ever have money enough to purchase a ticket.

March 3, we went on board the transport "General Sedgwick," bound for Annapolis. We pulled out near Fort Fisher and lay over night. Some of us went on shore at Smithfield and had a nice time. On the 4th we got under way. It was the second inauguration of President Lincoln, and all the ships were gaily decked with flags. We passed out over the bar. The ship was crowded; my berth was on the floor between decks. I find the last entry in my diary is, "Oh, how sick I am!" I did not come on deck for four days, and suffered more than I can tell. The sea broke over the ship, and the water came down the hatchway. A western officer, suffering near, aroused me by exclaiming, "My God! Jack, there is a board off somewhere; don't you see the water coming in?" I didn't care if they were all off.

Home

We arrived at Annapolis and quartered in the several hotels. The following day we received two months' pay. I bought a good uniform of a Jew for seventy-five dollars, it was a nice blue when I first put it on, but before I arrived home it was as brown as a butternut. We ate from six to ten meals a day for a week, then received thirty days' furlough and came home to friends who had almost given us up for dead.

I never looked better than when I arrived home. I had bloated so that I was the picture of health, and no matter what account I gave of prison life my face contradicted it, so I said little. After thirty days at home I did not feel able to return, and received an extension. The war was nearly over, Richmond had fallen, and I was miles away, a paroled prisoner, not allowed to bear arms until exchanged.

While at home I had the pleasure of meeting my old comrade, Isaac H. Boyd. He had started as a private in Company A, and was now major of the regiment. I left him one Saturday at the Providence depot in Boston, he returning to the front. In two weeks I received his body at the same depot. He was killed in the last battle of the war, the day before Lee surrendered,—one of the bravest officers who ever drew a sword.

Early in May I returned to Annapolis, and was pleasantly quartered in the house of a Mr. Harper, the only man in the city who voted for President Lincoln in 1860. While standing on the street one day, a small squad of prisoners passed. This was an unusual sight, as all had come through the lines weeks before. I heard a voice say, "How are you, captain?" and looking up saw a white head sticking out of a bundle of rags, and recognized Sergt. Mike Scannell. I said, "Mike, you are dead." "Not yet," was the reply; "but I have been mighty near it. I was sent out to die at Andersonville, from there was taken to Blackshire, Fla., kept until the war was over, then taken within several miles of our lines and turned loose." With him was Mike O'Brien of my company,—hard looking, but full of courage.

A Pleasant Command

On the 15th of May I was discharged by general order, went to Washington, received my full pay, with transportation to West Newbury, Mass. I waited to see the grand review of the

armies before returning home. The first day the Army of the
Potomac passed. As the 2d corps drew near I became anxious, and walked towards the Capitol. The white trefoil
came in sight, and at the head of the dear old regiment rode
Colonel Rice. He saw me and turned out of the line to shake
hands. Next came Captain Hume,—the only line officer
commissioned when we were captured. He stopped, and the
boys came from every company; for a few moments I held
a reception. Colonel Rice urged me to come to the regiment,
saying he had found a place for me. I informed him that I
was discharged, and was going home, but he said, "Come
and see me day after to-morrow." In compliance with his request I went out to Munson's Hill to visit the regiment, and
before night was mustered as captain, and assigned to the
command of Company B.

The duty was very pleasant. I was in command of the regiment a few days during the absence of Colonel Rice and
Captain Hume, and was two weeks on courts-martial detail.
June 30 the regiment was mustered out of service, and left
for Massachusetts, arriving at Readville July 3. We were invited to take part in the parade in Boston July 4, and Colonel
Rice was quite anxious that we should. After we went to our
quarters for dinner Colonel Rice was called to Boston. Nearly all the officers had business there, and when we boarded
the train found the men taken the same way. The colonel did
not blame them, and said it was all right if we would report
at 9 A.M. the next day at the Providence depot. All promised.
I did not expect they would come but went to the station at
the hour named. I found Colonel Rice and one private. We
waited a while, but no more reported, and as we three would
not make much of a show, concluded to give it up.

July 20 we assembled at Readville for final pay. The men
returned to their homes and took up the duties of citizens
which they had laid down to become soldiers,—and the 19th
Regiment Massachusetts Volunteers became a thing of the
past.

Advice from an Old Friend

Lydia Maria Child

With the ending of the Civil War, the abolitionists of the North saw a hard task to follow: the integration of the former slaves as free and equal members of society. Most could not have realized that this effort would take many decades and involve conflict, hatred, and suffering nearly equal to that of the Civil War itself.

Author Lydia Maria Child, in her article "Advice From an Old Friend," gives suggestions which she believed would smooth the transition to freedom for the country's emancipated slaves. Showing an earnest optimism, tinged with naïveté and what modern readers would consider condescension, Child explains that acceptance by whites will eventually come with the wearing of clean clothing, good manners, thriftiness, and the careful maintenance of a home and its garden.

For many years I have felt great sympathy for you, my brethren and sisters, and I have tried to do what I could to help you to freedom. And now that you have at last received the long-desired blessing, I most earnestly wish that you should make the best possible use of it. I have made this book to encourage you to exertion by examples of what colored people are capable of doing. Such men and women as Toussaint l'Ouverture, Benjamin Banneker, Phillis Wheatley, Frederick Douglass, and William and Ellen Crafts, prove that the power of *character* can overcome all external disadvantages, even that most crushing of all disadvantages, Slav-

Reprinted from Lydia Maria Child, "Advice from an Old Friend," in *The Freedmen's Book* (Boston: n.p., 1865).

ery. Perhaps few of you will be able to stir the hearts of large assemblies by such eloquent appeals as those of Frederick Douglass, or be able to describe what you have seen and heard so gracefully as Charlotte L. Forten does. Probably none of you will be called to govern a state as Toussaint L'Ouverture did; for such a remarkable career as his does not happen once in hundreds of years. But the Bible says, "He that ruleth his own spirit is greater than he that ruleth a kingdom"; and such a ruler every man and woman can become, by the help and blessing of God. It is not the *greatness* of the thing a man does which makes him worthy of respect; it is the doing *well* whatsoever he hath to do. In many respects, your opportunities for usefulness are more limited than those of others; but you have one great opportunity peculiar to yourselves. You can do a vast amount of good to people in various parts of the world, and through successive generations, by simply being sober, industrious, and honest. There are still many slaves in Brazil and in the Spanish possessions. If you are vicious, lazy, and careless, their masters will excuse themselves for continuing to hold them in bondage, by saying: "Look at the freedmen of the United States! What idle vagabonds they are! How dirty their cabins are! How slovenly their dress! That proves that negroes cannot take care of themselves, that they are not fit to be free." But if your houses look neat, and your clothes are clean and whole, and your gardens well weeded, and your work faithfully done, whether for yourselves or others, then all the world will cry out, "You see that negroes *can* take care of themselves; and it is a sin and a shame to keep such men in Slavery." Thus, while you are serving your own interests, you will be helping on the emancipation of poor weary slaves in other parts of the world. It is a great privilege to have a chance to do extensive good by such simple means, and your Heavenly Father will hold you responsible for the use you make of your influence.

Serious and Important Matters

Your manners will have a great effect in producing an impression to your advantage or disadvantage. Be always respectful and polite toward your associates, and toward those who have been in the habit of considering you an inferior race. It is one of the best ways to prove that you are not inferior. Never allow yourselves to say or do anything in the presence of women of your own color which it would be improper for you to say or do in the presence of the most refined white ladies. Such a course will be an education for them as well as for yourselves. When you appoint committees about your schools and other public affairs, it would be wise to have both men and women on the committees. The habit of thinking and talking about serious and important matters makes women more sensible and discreet. Such consultations together are in fact a practical school both for you and them; and the more modest and intelligent women are, the better will children be brought up.

Personal appearance is another important thing. It is not necessary to be rich in order to dress in a becoming manner. A pretty dress for festival occasions will last a long while, if well taken care of; and a few wild-flowers, or bright berries, will ornament young girls more tastefully than jewels. Working-clothes that are clean and nicely patched always look respectable; and they make a very favorable impression, because they indicate that the wearer is neat and economical. And here let me say, that it is a very great saving to mend garments well, and before the rents get large. We thrifty Yankees have a saying that "a stitch in time saves nine"; and you will find by experience that neglected mending will require more than nine stitches instead of one, and will not look so well when it is done.

The appearance of your villages will do much to produce a favorable opinion concerning your characters and capabilities. Whitewash is not expensive; and it takes but little time to transplant a cherokee rose, a jessamine, or other wild shrubs and vines that make the poorest cabin look beautiful; and, once planted, they will be growing while you are working or sleeping. It is a public benefit to remove everything dirty or unsightly, and to surround homes with verdure and flowers; for a succession of pretty cottages makes the whole road pleasant, and cheers all passers by; while they are at the same time an advertisement, easily read by all men, that the people who live there are not lazy, slovenly, or vulgar. The rich pay a great deal of money for pictures, to ornament their walls, but a whitewashed cabin, with flowering-shrubs and vines clustering round it, is a pretty picture freely exhibited to all men. It is a public benefaction.

But even if you are as yet too poor to have a house and garden of your own, it is still in your power to be a credit and an example to your race: by working for others as faithfully as you would work for yourself; by taking as good care of their tools as you would if they were your own; by always keeping your promises, however inconvenient it may be; by being strictly honest in all your dealings; by being temperate in your habits, and never speaking a profane or indecent word,—by pursuing such a course you will be consoled with an inward consciousness of doing right in the sight of God, and be a public benefactor by your example, while at the same time you will secure respect and prosperity for yourself by establishing a good character. A man whose conduct inspires confidence is in a fair way to have house and land of his own, even if he starts in the world without a single cent.

Money Matters

Be careful of your earnings, and as saving in your expenses as is consistent with health and comfort; but never allow yourself to be stingy. Avarice is a mean vice, which eats all the heart out of a man. Money is a good thing, and you ought to want to earn it, as a means of improving the condition of yourselves and families. But it will do good to your character, and increase your happiness, if you impart a portion of your earnings to others who are in need. Help as much as you conveniently can in building churches and school-houses for the good of all, and in providing for the sick and the aged. If your former masters and mistresses are in trouble, show them every kindness in your power, whether they have treated you kindly or not. Remember the words of the blessed Jesus: "Do good to them that hate you, and pray for them which despitefully use you and persecute you."

There is one subject on which I wish to guard you against disappointment. Do not be discouraged if freedom brings you more cares and fewer advantages than you expected. Such a great change as it is from Slavery to Freedom cannot be completed all at once. By being brought up as slaves, you have formed some bad habits, which it will take time to correct. Those who were formerly your masters have acquired still worse habits by being brought up as slaveholders; and they cannot be expected to change all at once. Both of you will gradually improve under the teaching of new circumstances. For a good while it will provoke many of them to see those who were once their slaves acting like freemen. They will doubtless do many things to vex and discourage you, just as the slaveholders in Jamaica did after emancipation there. They seemed to want to drive their emancipated bondmen to insurrection, that they might have a pretext for saying: "You see what a bad effect freedom has on negroes! We told you it would be so!" But the colored people of Jamaica behaved better than their former masters wished them to do. They left the plantations where they were badly treated, or poorly paid, but they worked diligently elsewhere. Their women and children raised vegetables and fowls and carried them to market; and, by their united industry and economy, they soon had comfortable little homes of their own.

Former Masters

I think it would generally be well for you to work for your former masters, if they treat you well, and pay you as much as you could earn elsewhere. But if they show a disposition to oppress you, quit their service, and work for somebody who will treat you like freemen. If they use violent language to you, never use impudent language to them. If they cheat you, scorn to cheat them in return. If they break their promises, never break yours. If they propose to women such connections as used to be common under the bad system of Slavery, teach them that freedwomen not only have the legal power to protect themselves from such degradation, but also that they have pride of character. If in fits of passion, they abuse your children as they formerly did, never revenge it by any injury to them or their property. It is an immense advantage to any man always to keep the right on his side. If you pursue this course you will always be superior, however rich or elegant may be the man or woman who wrongs you.

I do not mean by this that you ought to submit tamely to insult or oppression. Stand up for your rights, but do it in a manly way. Quit working for a man who speaks to you contemptuously, or tries to take a mean advantage of you, when you are doing your duty faithfully by him. If it becomes necessary, apply to magistrates to protect you and redress your wrongs. If you are so unlucky as to live where the men in authority, whether civil or military, are still disposed to treat the colored people as slaves, let the most intelligent among you draw up a statement of your grievances and send it to some of your firm friends in Congress, such as the Hon. Charles Sumner, the Hon. Henry Wilson, and the Hon. George W. Julian.

A good government seeks to make laws that will equally protect and restrain all men. Heretofore you had no reason to respect the laws of this country, because they punished you for crime, in many cases more severely than white men were punished, while they did nothing to protect your rights. But now that good President Lincoln has made you free, you will be legally protected in your rights and restrained from doing wrong, just as other men are protected and restrained. It is one of the noblest privileges of freemen to be able to respect the law, and to rely upon it always for redress of grievances, instead of revenging one wrong by another wrong.

You will have much to put up with before the new order of things can become settled on a permanent foundation. I am grieved to read in the newspapers how wickedly you are still treated in some places; but I am not surprised, for I knew that Slavery was a powerful snake, that would try to do mischief with its tail after its head was crushed. But, whatever wrongs you may endure, comfort yourselves with two reflections: first, that there is the beginning of a better state of things, from which your children will derive much more benefit than you can; secondly, that a great majority of the American people are sincerely determined that you shall be protected in your rights as freemen. Year by year your condition will improve. Year by year, if you respect yourselves, you will be more and more respected by white men. Wonderful changes have taken place in your favor during the last thirty years, and the changes are still going on. The Abolitionist did a great deal for you, by their continual writing and preaching against Slavery. Then this war enabled thousands of people to see for themselves what a bad institution Slavery was; and the uniform kindness with which you treated the Yankee soldiers raised you up multitudes of friends. There are still many pro-slavery people in the Northern States, who, from aristocratic pride or low vulgarity, still call colored people "niggers," and treat them as such. But the good leaven is now fairly worked into public sentiment, and these people, let them do what they will, cannot get it out.

The providence of God has opened for you an upward path. Walk ye in it, without being discouraged by the brambles and stones at the outset. Those who come after you will clear them away, and will place in their stead strong, smooth rails for the steam-car called Progress of the Colored Race.

Chronology

1820
The Missouri Compromise is reached after a bitter debate over the issue of slavery in a new state. Slavery is to be barred north of a latitude paralleling the southern border of Missouri.

1832
South Carolina attempts to nullify federal tariffs, defying the authority of Congress.

1850
After the application of California to join the Union, the Compromise of 1850 is reached in Congress. The legislation admits California as a free state; New Mexico and Utah are organized as territories with the residents of each to decide on slavery. A Fugitive Slave Act is passed in an attempt to hinder runaway slaves.

1852
Harriet Beecher Stowe's antislavery novel *Uncle Tom's Cabin* whips up abolitionist sentiment in the North.

1854
The Kansas-Nebraska Act permits the population of new territories to decide whether or not to permit slavery within their borders.

1857
March 6: In the *Dred Scott* decision, the Supreme Court denies the petition of a slave for his freedom on the grounds that blacks are not citizens and do not lose their status as slaves even when taken into free territory. The Court also rules that Congress could not legally bar slavery in new territories.

1858
Abraham Lincoln and Stephen Douglas draw national attention to a series of debates over slavery and states' rights in Illinois.

1859
October 16: Abolitionist John Brown stages an unsuccessful raid on the federal arsenal at Harpers Ferry, Virginia, in an attempt to spark a slave rebellion. Brown is hanged December 2 after being convicted of treason.

1860
November 4: Abraham Lincoln is elected president, pledging to bar slavery in new territories.

December 20: South Carolina passes the Ordinances of Secession and withdraws from the Union.

1861
January–February: Six more Southern states join South Carolina and secede from the Union.

February–March: Delegates from seceding states draw up a Constitution and elect Jefferson Davis as president and form the Confederate States of America.

March 4: Lincoln is sworn in as the 16th president.

April 12: Confederate batteries bombard Fort Sumter in Charleston harbor, touching off the Civil War.

April 15: Lincoln issues his first call for volunteers to fight for the Union.

April 19: Lincoln proclaims a naval blockade of Southern ports.

May 21: The Confederate States of America moves its capital to Richmond, Virginia.

July 21: Confederate troops force Union troops to retreat at First Manassas (Bull Run).

1862
February 6: General Ulysses S. Grant captures Fort Henry, Tennessee, from Confederate troops.

March 9: The ironclad ships *Monitor* from the North, and *Merrimac* from the South, clash. The battle ends in a draw.

April 25: New Orleans falls to a Union fleet under the command of David Farragut and is placed under Union occupation.

May 31: Union and Confederate armies fight at Seven Pines, Virginia. The Confederate commander of the Army of Virginia, Joseph Johnston, is wounded and replaced by Robert E. Lee.

June 25–July 1: Lee saves Richmond from a Union advance in the Seven Days' battles.

August 29 and 30: The Union army is defeated by Lee and Jackson at Second Manassas.

September 17: The Battle of Antietam, near Sharpsburg, Maryland, turns back a Confederate invasion of the North. The North suffered 12,000 casualties, while the South lost 13,000—the bloodiest day of the war.

September 22: After the victory at Antietam, Lincoln issues a preliminary Emancipation Proclamation, which will take effect January 1, 1863.

December 13: Entrenched Confederate forces repulse a Union charge at the Battle of Fredericksburg, inflicting heavy losses.

1863

January 1: The Emancipation Proclamation takes effect.

March 3: The United States Congress passes the first conscription law.

May 2: Grant begins a siege of Vicksburg, Mississippi, the last Confederate stronghold on the Mississippi River.

May 2–4: Lee defeats a Union army at Chancellorsville, during which Stonewall Jackson, a leading Confederate general, is mortally wounded by friendly fire.

July 1–3: Lee's Army of Northern Virginia engages the Army of the Potomac under General George Meade. The Union forces stand fast against furious Confederate charges, stopping the Confederate campaign in southern Pennsylvania. This battle ended the last major Confederate offensive of the war.

July 4: Vicksburg surrenders to Grant.

September 19 and 20: A Union army under General W.S. Rosecrans is beaten at Chickamauga, northern Georgia.

November 19: Lincoln delivers the Gettysburg Address.

1864
March 9: Ulysses S. Grant is appointed overall commander of the Union forces.

May 5 and 6: Confederate and Union troops fight to a stalemate at the Battle of the Wilderness.

June 3: A Union assault at Cold Harbor is stopped by a strong Confederate defense.

June 20: Grant begins a siege of Petersburg in southern Virginia.

September 2: Atlanta falls after a Union bombardment.

November 8: Lincoln is re-elected as president, promising to see the Union effort through.

December 21: After a scorched-earth march through Georgia, General William Sherman captures Savannah.

1865
April 3: Grant captures Petersburg, Virginia, forcing the evacuation of Richmond.

April 9: Lee surrenders at Appomattox Courthouse, Virginia.

April 14: Lincoln is assassinated in Washington, D.C., by John Wilkes Booth, a Confederate sympathizer. Andrew Johnson becomes president.

April 26: Confederate general Johnston surrenders to General Sherman at Raleigh, ending the Civil War.

December 13: The states ratify the Thirteenth Amendment to the Constitution, abolishing slavery.

For Further Research

Bruce Catton, *The Civil War*. Boston: Houghton Mifflin, 1987.

———, *This Hallowed Ground: The Story of the Union Side in the Civil War*. Garden City, NY: Doubleday, 1956.

Clinton Cox, *Undying Glory: The Story of the 54th Massachusetts Regiment*. New York: Scholastic, 1991.

Richard Nelson Current, *Lincoln's Loyalists: Union Soldiers from the Confederacy*. Boston: Northeastern University Press, 1992.

Burke Davis, *Sherman's March: The First Full-Length Narrative of General William Tecumseh Sherman's Devastating March Through Georgia and the Carolinas*. New York: Vintage, 1988.

Kenneth C. Davis, *Don't Know Much About the Civil War: Everything You Need to Know About America's Greatest Conflict but Never Learned*. New York: Avon, 1997.

William C. Davis, *Lincoln's Men: How President Lincoln Became Father to an Army and a Nation*. New York: Touchstone, 1999.

Luis F. Emilio, *A Brave Black Regiment: The History of the 54th Massachusetts, 1863–1865*. New York: Da Capo, 1995.

Shelby Foote, *The Civil War: A Narrative*. New York: Vintage, 1986.

Webb Garrison, *Civil War Curiosities: Strange Stories, Oddities, Events, and Coincidences*. Nashville, TN: Rutledge Hill, 1994.

Harry Hansen, *The Civil War: A History*. New York: Mentor, 1961.

Donald Dale Jackson, *Twenty Million Yankees: The Northern Home Front*. Alexandria, VA: Time-Life, 1985.

Clint Johnson, *Civil War Blunders*. Winston-Salem, NC: John F. Blair, 1997.

Archer Jones, *Civil War Command and Strategy: The Process of Victory and Defeat*. New York: Free, 1992.

C. Brian Kelly, *Best Little Stories from the Civil War*. Nashville, TN: Cumberland House, 1998.

Robert Leckie, *None Died in Vain: The Saga of the American Civil War*. New York: Harper & Row, 1990.

Larry M. Logue, *To Appomattox and Beyond: The Civil War Soldier in War and Peace*. Chicago: I.R. Dee, 1996.

Walter Lowenfels, ed., *Walt Whitman's Civil War*. New York: Da Capo, n.d.

Mary Elizabeth Massey, *Women in the Civil War*. Lincoln: University of Nebraska Press, 1966.

James M. McPherson, *For Cause and Comrades: Why Men Fought in the Civil War*. New York: Oxford University Press, 1997.

———, *Marching Toward Freedom: Blacks in the Civil War, 1861–1865*. New York: Facts On File, 1991.

W. Springer Menge and J. August Shimrak, eds., *The Civil War Notebook of Daniel Chishom: A Chronicle of Daily Life in the Union Army, 1864–1865*. New York: Orion, 1989.

Frances Trevelyan Miller, ed., *Prisons and Hospitals*. New York: Castle, 1957.

Joseph E. Persico, *My Enemy, My Brother: Men and Days of Gettysburg*. New York: Da Capo, 1996.

Delia Ray, *Behind the Blue and Gray: The Soldier's Life in the Civil War*. New York: Lodestar, 1991.

Michael Shaara, *The Killer Angels*. New York: Random House, 1993.

Kenneth M. Stampp, ed., *The Causes of the Civil War*. New York: Touchstone, 1986.

James L. Stokesbury, *A Short History of the Civil War.* New York: W. Morrow, 1995.

George Sullivan, *Matthew Brady: His Life and Photographs.* New York: Cobblehill, 1994.

Warren Wilkinson, *Mother, May You Never See the Sights I Have Seen: The 57th Massachusetts Veteran Volunteers.* New York: Harper & Row, 1990.

Steven E. Woodworth, ed., *Civil War Generals in Defeat.* Lawrence: University Press of Kansas, 1999.

Mike Wright, *What They Didn't Teach You About the Civil War.* Novato, CA: Presidio, 1996.

Index